T0330453

Business Creation

Dedicated to

Nancy Carter and Bill Gartner,
who were instrumental in initiating the Entrepreneurial Research
Consortium
that made the U.S. PSED I possible

and

Richard Curtin,
who supervised the creation, documentation and dissemination
of the PSED I and II data sets,
facilitating wide use by the research community.

Business Creation

Ten Factors for Entrepreneurial Success

Paul D. Reynolds

USA

Edward **Elgar**
PUBLISHING

Cheltenham, UK • Northampton, MA, USA

© Paul D. Reynolds 2018

All rights reserved. No part of this publication may be reproduced, stored in a retrieval system or transmitted in any form or by any means, electronic, mechanical or photocopying, recording, or otherwise without the prior permission of the publisher.

Published by
Edward Elgar Publishing Limited
The Lypiatts
15 Lansdown Road
Cheltenham
Glos GL50 2JA
UK

Edward Elgar Publishing, Inc.
William Pratt House
9 Dewey Court
Northampton
Massachusetts 01060
USA

A catalogue record for this book
is available from the British Library

Library of Congress Control Number: 2018944792

This book is available electronically in the **Elgar**online
Business subject collection
DOI 10.4337/9781788118354

ISBN 978 1 78811 834 7 (cased)
ISBN 978 1 78811 835 4 (eBook)

Typeset by Servis Filmsetting Ltd, Stockport, Cheshire
Printed and bound by CPI Group (UK) Ltd, Croydon CR0 4YY

Contents

Preface

Many people are attracted to entrepreneurship. Some relish the idea of instant wealth, others see promising business opportunities, being their own boss appeals to many, and some find that satisfying work for others is difficult to locate—or tolerate. Whatever their motives, the numbers involved are substantial: at any given time tens of millions in North America and Europe are trying to start new firms—world-wide there are over a quarter of a billion.

Responding to this interest, a wide variety of programs, books, websites, seminars, weekend workshops, college courses, reality television and the like have emerged to facilitate business creation. Many are based on personal experience or knowledge of specific industries or the latest internet based technology. All strongly encourage others to pursue business creation; none offers to share the risks. This is consistent with the emphasis of policy makers. National, regional, and local politicians expect more entrepreneurship to increase economic growth; they rarely acknowledge the social costs.

Despite this great surge of attention there has been a lack of precision about the nature of the start-up process, which may mislead nascent entrepreneurs. While there is a substantial literature on various features of business creation, most are based on samples of convenience, cross sectional analysis, or administrative data sets that have limited information about the activities involved in business creation.

The Panel Study of Entrepreneurial Dynamics (PSED) projects have done much to fill this void. These efforts begin with a representative sample of the adult population and identify those active in business creation. This cohort then completes detailed interviews over a number of years, allowing tracking of the outcome of their efforts. The result is a description of the activities and events that occur during the start-up process for both initiatives that become profitable as well as those that are discontinued. It facilitates identifying major features of the entrepreneurial process associated with a successful outcome.

Based on the data from two U.S. PSED cohorts, this volume describes the major features of firm creation. This review of a complex, multifaceted phenomenon is organized around ten "statements of fact." The focus is on empirical support for the relationships between major features of the business creation process and the outcomes, emphasizing ventures that reach profitability. These have implications for both those pursuing entrepreneurship as well as those developing public policies to facilitate business creation.

The initial objective was to provide an overview of the major features of business creation, using the U.S. PSED I and II data sets with the appropriate case weights. The first version was completed in August 2017, using case weights adjusted for biases in sampling and the start-up team size. Soon after an assessment by Shim and Davidsson (2018) provided a strategy for additional weight adjustments that would compensate for the considerable variation among nascent ventures in the time spent in the start-up process. This compensates for the identification of the ventures at an arbitrary point in the start-up process.

Preliminary assessments using these "triple adjusted" case weights (discussed in the Appendix) made clear that this dramatically affected most descriptions of business creation, particularly the proportions with different outcomes. The proportion of profitable businesses was increased from one-fourth to over one-third, offset by a reduction of those "still active." As a consequence, production of the book was placed on hold and the entire analysis was revised during the winter of 2018. This may be the first comprehensive description of business creation using these more appropriate nascent venture case weights.

The impact of these revised case weights cannot be overstated. While virtually every description related to nascent ventures' outcomes has been affected by the revised weights, the impact was substantial in presenting the structure of the start-up teams (Chapter 5), the amount of informal and formal funding (Chapters 9 and 10), and the time required to reach an outcome (Chapter 11). This makes clear that any analysis of representative samples of start-up nascent ventures that is not adjusted to compensate for duration in the business creation process may be very misleading.

If this overview reduces the personal and social cost associated with gaining the benefits of business creation, it will have been a success.

Paul D. Reynolds
Steamboat Springs, Colorado
May 2018

1. Introduction

On October 28, 2003 Harvard students could use "Facemash" to compare which photos of two undergraduates were "hot" or "not hot." Developed as personal project by Mark Zuckerberg it was followed by several other efforts that led to the implementation of "Thefacebook" on February 4, 2004; this provided students a mechanism for internet based social interaction. A five person start-up team embellished the potential for interaction and expanded access to other universities, high schools and eventually anybody over 13 years old. When the first public offering was initiated in 2012, "Facebook" reported annual revenue of $5 billion, yearly profits of $53 million, one billion users, and 4,619 employees.[1]

Convinced that a properly designed website could provide an efficient and economical interface between citizens and government agencies, high school buddies Kaleil Tuzman and Tom Herman used seed money from Herman's mother to implement "Govworks.com" to process parking tickets in May 1999. A four person start-up team led the website development and within 18 months "Govworks.com" raised $70 million to support 250 employees. Out maneuvered by competitors such as "ezgov.com," unable to manage the complex technical issues, and confronted with a dramatic decline in stock market valuations of internet based initial public offerings, by January 2001 the remnants of the firm were sold for $12 million.[2]

In 2003 a team of three men and one women began developing "Southeast Foundations Are Us," which would prepare building sites for new construction. They anticipated a firm that would be easy to manage and have 25 employees in five years. Within two and a half years they became profitable; two years later they had sales of $2.4 million and ten full-time employees.[3]

In 2005 two sisters worked on creating "Mountain States Jewelry of Distinction," hoping to have annual sales of $300,000 in five years with an easy to manage business. Within four months the store reached profitability and in two years the sisters and three employees had an annual revenue of $264,000. Sales declined to $120,000 in the third year and the store was shut down.[4]

Business creation takes many forms with many outcomes. Facebook is a well-known example that went from zero to a billion users in nine years. Less well known is Startup.com. Initiated in 1999 it burned through $70 million in venture capital funds and never came close to profitability in 21 months. Southeast Foundations represents a more modest effort that appears to be on track to become a successful part of the construction industry. Mountain States Jewelry of Distinction had two years of success, but in the third year the founders disengaged. These real-life examples are interesting, but do not provide clear implications for those seeking to create a new business.

In the early 1990s a great deal of research provided important new information about market economies—entrepreneurship and new firm creation were a major source of growth and adaptations. In addition, there was growing evidence that a substantial minority of those in the workforce were attracted to business creation. But other than a wealth of individual success stories and analyses reflecting samples of convenience, there was little systematic information about the nature of those involved in business creation or the basic features of the process. This led to the development of a research program that involved the identification of representative samples of those active in business creation and tracking their progress and outcomes. Since 1995 this research protocol, the Panel Study of Entrepreneurial Dynamics (PSED), has now been implemented in a dozen countries and the resulting data sets have been used to explore a wide range of entrepreneurial phenomena.

A precise understanding of firm creation begins with a conceptualization of the phenomena. Business creation is the beginning of the business life course, represented in Figure 1.1.

Businesses are created by people. This conception assumes those individuals do so on their own, as nascent entrepreneurs, or as they work for an existing business, nascent intrapreneurs. Over half of nascent ventures are team efforts; more than one person expects to own the new firm. There are two important transitions in the initial stages of the firm life course: entry into the start-up process and firm birth. Firm birth reflecting the shift from a nascent venture to a new firm. As will be seen, the majority of nascent ventures complete a third transition. They are terminated before they become new firms, represented by the "quit" arrow in Figure 1.1. The entire process exists in a unique political, social, economic and historical context, which can vary dramatically between countries and among regions within a country.

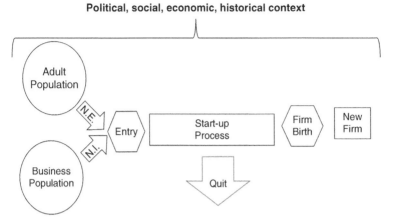

Political, social, economic, historical context

N.E. = Nascent Entrepreneur; N.I. = Nascent Intrapreneur

Figure 1.1   Conception of the start-up process

The firm life course may be complicated. The start-up period may be brief, intense, and hectic or it may take years of trial and error development to arrive at a useful product or service. Precise descriptions of the process are complicated by the lack of agreement on the criteria for identifying the transitions and different types of businesses.[5] For the following discussion, beginning the start-up process is defined as the date of the first of two activities initiated within 12 months. A firm birth is considered the first occurrence of profits, identified as the beginning of a period of positive monthly cash flow.

These rich descriptions of the start-up process provide a great deal of systematic information about the business creation experience. Information very relevant for those considering or involved in business creation. They also provide substantial evidence relevant to adjusting public policy to facilitate entrepreneurial activity.

These "lessons learned" can be summarized as ten statements, provided in Table 1.1.

The following reviews the best available evidence related to these ten issues from representative samples of those active in U.S. business creation. These samples reflect the patterns to be expected by 16 million nascent entrepreneurs working on ten million nascent ventures.

Table 1.1   Ten things to know about business creation

1	It can be very satisfying.
2	Everybody gets involved; some more than others.
3	Motives are diverse and may change.
4	It is a social experience.
5	Know what you are doing.
6	Do it!
7	Some activities are more helpful than others.
8	It takes some effort.
9	Money may be necessary, but is not sufficient.
10	Profits are elusive, prepare to pivot.

The focus on these relationships reflect an assumption that those considering business creation:

● Seek to implement a venture that will become profitable or economically self-sustaining.
● Wish to minimize the costs of reaching profitability.
● Would like to reduce the cost in time and money of identifying a still-born venture, one that would not become profitable.

While the focus of the assessment is on commercial or for-profit new ventures, the basic patterns are applicable to those seeking to implement not-for-profit initiatives to achieve social objectives. Such efforts must be economically viable to have a social impact.

It is assumed that policy makers seek to gain the advantages of firm creation—increased productivity, job creation, and the adaptation and creation of economic sectors. But, as shown in Chapter 9, start-up activity involves substantial costs in time and money. Almost all of this cost is borne by the start-up teams and about half by teams that do not reach profitability. This reflects the low proportion of start-up efforts, about two-fifths, that achieve profitability. Policy makers are confronted with a dilemma: efforts to increase business creation will increase the social costs. But without more new firms, there will be less job creation, less improved productivity, and less innovation.

The major relationships discussed in the following chapters will be considered in terms of several policy related issues.

- What actions may increase participation in business creation?
- What actions may increase the proportion of nascent ventures that reach profitability?
- What actions may reduce the social costs associated with business creation?

Given that the majority of start-up efforts are abandoned, small gains in the proportion that become profitable can lead to major increases in benefit versus cost ratios.

NOTES

1. Summary based on SEC Form 10-K filing (U.S. Securities and Exchange Commission, 2013) and public access summary of the firm's history (Wikipedia, 2013).
2. Based on close viewing of the movie, *Startup.com* (Hegedus and Noujaim, 2001) and related commentaries (Steiner, 2010; Writers Institute, undated).
3. U.S. PSED II case number 51609; fictitious firm name.
4. U.S. PSED II case number 51578; fictitious firm name.
5. The diverse interpretations that emerge from different theoretical and operational definitions of "firm birth" are explored in Reynolds (2017).

2. It can be very satisfying

> ... there is the joy of creating, of getting things done, or simply of exercising one's energy and ingenuity. (Schumpeter 1934, p. 93)

> The entrepreneurial life is one of challenge, work, dedication, perseverance, exhilaration, agony, accomplishment, failure, sacrifice, control, powerlessness ... but ultimately, extraordinary satisfaction. (Start-up angel investor, David S. Rose, 2014)

People that start successful businesses are among the most satisfied in the economy. The billionaire entrepreneurs featured in the media are clearly pleased with their success and attention, brimming with self-confidence and optimism. Perhaps even more significant is the growing body of research indicating that business owners and entrepreneurs are more satisfied with their work careers than wage and salary workers; this is true at all levels of occupational sophistication.

Examples of the satisfaction from creating a profitable business are described below:

Mary (26 years old) is very satisfied with the experience of working with four partners, three men (30, 53 and 38 years old) and one other woman (50 years old). All with five to 35 years of work experience and two who had been involved in three or more start-ups. They joined the effort with equal shares in a new pet boarding business and planned on maximizing growth by serving local customers. Noticing a strong demand for the service at the same time as an interest in business creation developed, the team began to develop the business idea. Six months later work began on a business plan, including defining the market to be served, creating financial projections, organizing the start-up team, and investing personal funds in the development of the business. After 12 months, promotion of the venture was initiated, capital assets were acquired, supplies were purchased (some with supplier credit), external funding was pursued, and the chief operating officer began to devote full-time to the business. After 24 months employees were hired and income was received from providing the services. By 40 months the monthly income covered recurring expenses and the salaries of the owner–management team. At last contact the firm had 23 employees and appeared to have a promising future. Mary, who had moved into the state three years before getting involved in business creation, has many reasons to be very satisfied with her life.[1]

Roger and Rachel are a married couple, raising four teenagers, and have lived in the same state their whole lives. Roger benefited from 25 years of restaurant experience and Rachel has a long work history. They wanted independence and a good living and purchased an existing facility to create a specialty restaurant, the only one in their area. They expected three-fourths of their customers to be local and the rest from the region. They designed an equal partnership to implement a business that would be easy to manage. They expected to grow to 18 employees in five years. In the first month they developed a business plan, created a model for the business, defined their customer base, obtained an Employer Identification Number (EIN), organized the start-up team and began investing their own funds. The next month they began promotion and developing financial projections. In the fourth month they started hiring staff, purchasing property, developing supplier credit and ordering supplies, working full-time in the restaurant and receiving income. By the eighth month they had positive cash flow that covered all expenses and the owners' salaries. At the last report, the annual sales were half a million and they had two dozen employees. The results have been very high work satisfaction and satisfaction with life.[2]

These types of experiences underlie the dramatic differences between the work satisfaction of typical adults and those active in the business creation process. The satisfaction of nascent entrepreneurs is compared to those in wage and salary work in Figure 2.1.

As shown, over half (53%) of those active as nascent entrepreneurs are very or somewhat satisfied, compared to less than one-fifth (19%) of those in wage and salary work. The proportions that are dissatisfied is almost the reverse, as over two-thirds (71%) of wage and salary workers are somewhat or very dissatisfied compared to one-fourth (25%) of active nascent entrepreneurs.

Most people, over half, that get involved in business creation do not reach profitability. What about those that give up? The story of Denise is typical.

Denise, a 44-year-old African-American woman had lived in the inner city for 44 years, completed post-high vocational training and had 15 years of word processing experience. She noticed that this type of business service was not present in her neighborhood and thought there would be considerable local interest. She started her effort to create a business by promoting her availability to provide computer services. After several months, she was starting to define the customer base and by the second year had some customers and began preparation of a business

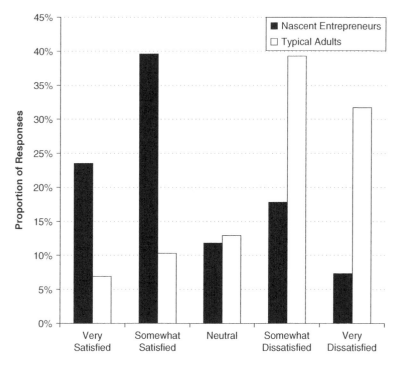

Figure 2.1   Work satisfaction: nascent entrepreneurs versus typical adults[3]

plan that included financial projections. After 44 months and limited revenue she shut down this venture and focused her efforts on a different start-up business. Denise was, however, satisfied with this experience and very happy with her life overall.[4]

While most that pursue business creation are more satisfied than typical workers, the outcome does have an effect, as shown in Figure 2.2. While four-fifths (84%) of those that have reached initial profitability are very or somewhat satisfied, it is still over half for those that have quit (58%) or are still active in the start-up process (67%). Remarkably, three times as many discouraged nascent entrepreneurs reflect high satisfaction as typical adults with jobs (57% versus 17%).[5]

The finding that those that are self-employed are more satisfied with their work is so well established that research has focused on

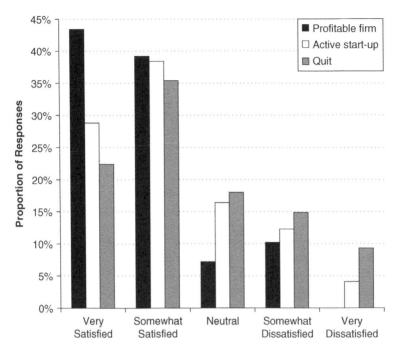

Figure 2.2   Nascent entrepreneur's satisfaction by outcome[6]

why this is the case. It may be that those "happy in their work" may be more likely to pursue firm creation, as implied by Figure 2.2. But the perception of autonomy and procedural freedom, or the ability to control one's own work activities, appears in virtually all studies as the major reason those managing their own businesses are more satisfied, even when age, gender, type of work, and personality factors are taken into account.[7] This higher satisfaction is present despite some evidence that those who own their own businesses may receive less in terms of financial rewards.

IT IS NOT FOR EVERYBODY

While about one in 20 adults in the United States are active in business creation at any given time, the other 19 are not. In fact, over their work career, two in five of men (41%) participate in some form of self-employment while three in five (59%) do not.[8] Starting a business typically involves a year of effort and tens of thousands of dollars that is lost forever if the venture does not achieve profitability, and over half do not reach this benchmark. While most that pursue new venture creation do so while they keep their day job, it is still a period of intense work, uncertainty, and some personal stress.

But business creation is not for everybody. Even in the United States, with millions involved in business creation, half of men complete their work career without a period of self-employment—and with no regrets. Further, in many advanced countries substantial support has developed for those that do not choose to work or create a new business—an extensive safety net. In such countries only a small proportion of the adult population pursue business creation. Business creation is so rare in some countries that many adults have never known an entrepreneur. A major result is they do not encourage their children to pursue business creation.

There is no question that creating a successful business can be very rewarding, even exhilarating, but for many others traditional work careers may be a better option.

OVERVIEW

Among those that get involved in business creation, it is clear that:

- Being involved is highly satisfying.
- Developing a profitable business is a very positive experience.
- Those that quit a start-up are more satisfied than typical wage and salary workers.
- It is not a comfortable career option for many.

The following chapters review major issues associated with business creation.

POLICY IMPLICATIONS

Many individuals find salary and wage work acceptable; others find satisfaction in pursuing business creation. At a minimum, public policy and programs should treat both options equally. The public education systems, both secondary and post-secondary, are generally organized to prepare most students for wage and salary work. Expansion of entrepreneurship training in post-secondary institutions is helping to make new workers more aware of all their career options. An expansion in secondary school curriculums would provide more young people with information about the entrepreneurial option, which they may find rewarding.

Increasing the proportion of workers that are business owners can increase overall job satisfaction, a major benefit for society.

NOTES

1. PSED I RESPID 328100140; fictitious name.
2. PSED I RESPID 328100268, fictitious names.
3. Based on the U.S. PSED I data set, with screening of representative samples of adults to identify typical wage and salary workers and nascent entrepreneurs in 1999, follow-ups completed at 14, 28, and 42 months. Items discussed in Johnson, Arthaud-Day, Rode, and Near (2004). Based on responses to QI8 in the first wave mail questionnaires completed by 507 nascent entrepreneurs and 350 comparison group respondents. Weights adjusted for screening sample biases.
4. PSED I RESPID 337800080; fictitious name.
5. Based on very or somewhat satisfied working adults in Figure 2.1 and entrepreneurs that have quit from Figure 2.2.
6. Based on last mail questionnaire available for each case from PSED I, items RI8, SI8, or TI8 and cases with known outcome status. Case weights adjusted for sampling screening and duration in process biases (n=399).
7. Blanchflower and Oswald (1998); Lange (2012).
8. See Reynolds (2007) Figure 11.1, p. 13.

3.   Everybody gets involved; some more than others

Who gets involved in business creation? *Everybody*. No one is excluded. Those involved include men and women of all ages, from all ethnic groups, and from all backgrounds. At any given time, about 16.3 million, 9.5 million men and 6.8 million women, are involved in trying to start a new business in the United States. As the typical start-up is a team effort, this is about 9.8 million business ventures. Two issues are relevant. The tendency of different individuals to get involved and the absolute number that are active. The bars in Figure 3.1 represent participation rates, number per 100, and the line the total counts, from 200,000 to 2.4 million.

As shown by the bars, participation is about twice as high for men compared to women. The most active group are men 35 to 44 years old, about one in eight (12%) are active in business creation. The most active women are their age peers, but only one in 12 (8%) are involved. At the other extreme are those men and women 65 to 74 years old, where one in 35 (2.9%) are nascent entrepreneurs. While this is 4% of the total, it does represent hundreds of thousands of individuals.

Examples of participation in business creation include:

Marsha and Bill, both in their 40s, were the major and equal partners, along with two other experienced men as junior partners, in establishing a business to prepare construction sites. This was the first start-up for everybody on the team, although all the men had several decades of experience in construction. They hoped for a firm that would be easy to manage and perhaps have a dozen employees and $3 million in sales five years after it was established. Work on the start-up began with developing a business plan and defining the local, regional, and national markets in which they would compete. Shortly after, they began to invest personal funds in the venture, a total of $50,000 for the four owners. Four months later they started to promote the new venture, including a phone line and website, acquired an EIN number and the start-up team organized the business operation. After one

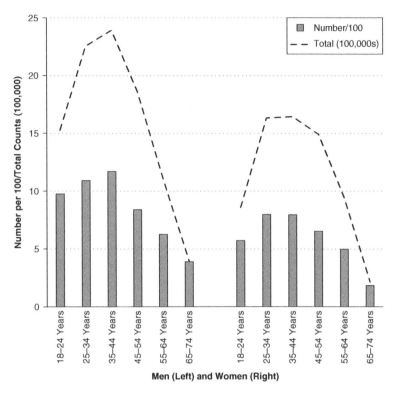

Figure 3.1   Participation in business creation by age and gender[1]

year they were developing financial projections and seeking outside funding, which they received, as well as developing supplier credit, and completed their first sales. Two years after beginning the process capital assets were acquired, materials and supplies were purchased, and the first employees hired. Thirty months after starting the process the new business was profitable.[2]

John, 73, and wife Sara, 45, have lived in the county for ten years. John has a lifetime of work experience and Sara 15 years as a beautician. They hoped to establish a profitable beauty shop that would be easy to manage, providing autonomy and income as they served local customers. They began by developing credit with suppliers and after a year began to promote the business. Although they have spent a thousand hours and $50,000 on the start-up, after ten years it is still not profitable. They are, nevertheless, not dissatisfied with the venture and are reasonably satisfied with their life situation.[3]

Thirty-year old Harry had 13 years of work experience and seven in the wholesale tire business. He decided to start his own operation, which he expected to be an easy to manage $3 million a year business with five employees; this would provide independence and financial security. After the idea developed he spend the first month on the business plan, defining markets and making financial projections. In the next two months Harry developed a model for the business, began to promote the business, hired an employee, developed supplier credit, asked for funding, and invested his own funds. By the seventh month he was able to secure capital assets and establish a dedicated phone and internet presence. Unfortunately, after 19 months and confronting a lack of customers, Harry shut down the effort and started a new job.[4]

Ethnic background is associated with participation in U.S. business creation. As shown in Figure 3.2, African-Americans and Hispanics

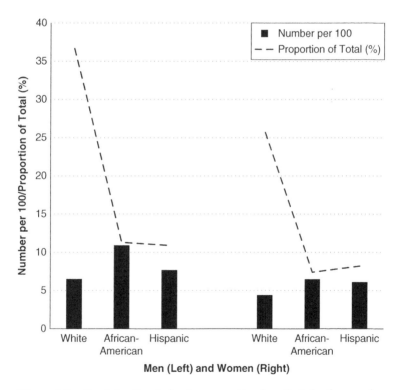

Figure 3.2   Participation in business creation by ethnic background and gender[5]

are more active than their White peers. However, because there are more Whites in the U.S. they account for the majority of nascent entrepreneurs. About 37% are White men and 26% are White women. Ethnic minority men are about 22% of the total, 11% African American, and 11% Hispanic. Ethnic minority women are about 16% of the total, about 8% for African-Americans and 8% for Hispanics.[6] Typical minority participation is illustrated by the following:

Leroy, a 36-year-old African-American had lived all his life in the same county and attended community college. After four years' experience as an insurance agent he saw strong customer demand. With support from the insurance company he decided to start his own agency, initially working out of his home. Although he was the sole owner, he called it the Macon and Macon Agency. He invested about 200 hours to get started, and in the first month got organized and invested some personal funds. After four months, he began to define the market, and after six months developed a business plan, began to promote and advertise, and had his first sales. Leasing capital assets and the purchase of supplies began after one year. In the beginning of the third year the agency was profitable and Leroy developed financial projections and registered the new firm.[7]

Maria and Jose, American born Hispanics, were in their mid-30s and both had two decades of experience in the auto repair business. They considered this a market with growing demand and the ability for bilingual service a competitive advantage. As equal partners, they planned to develop a growth business that would provide independence, flexibility to care for their children, and better security than their previous jobs. They began slowly, initially securing supplier credit. After four months, they had their first paying customer and after six months were developing a business model, defining the customer base, procuring supplies, acquiring capital assets, investing personal funds, and organizing the business. In the second year of the start-up process they hired employees, developed a business plan, and promoted the business. Monthly profitability occurred 16 months after starting the process.[8]

As with start-ups initiated by the majority, most ethnic minority ventures do not reach profitability, but these examples are typical of those that are successful.

READINESS FOR ENTREPRENEURSHIP

Focusing on the issue of who gets involved in business creation, the extent to which individuals are prepared to pursue firm creation is

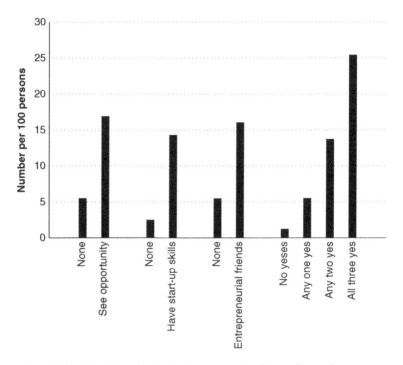

Figure 3.3   *Participation in business creation by readiness for*
            entrepreneurship[9]

an important issue. Large scale surveys completed in countries all over the world indicate that three personal factors, aside from age and gender, have a major impact. Those that recognize good business opportunities, are confident in their skills to manage new firm creation, and know other entrepreneurs are much more likely to be involved in business creation. The participation among those with these attributes, and a simple index reflecting the combination of these attributes is presented in Figure 3.3.

Each factor has a major impact on participating in business creation. Perception of a business opportunity increases participation by a factor of three. Those that have confidence in their start-up skills are six times as likely to be involved. And knowing others starting businesses triples the rate of participation. But the cumulative impact of these three factors is dramatic, as those reporting all three are 20 times as likely (25 per 100) to be involved in business creation compared to those with none of these characteristics (1.2 per 100). Among those active in business creation, 41% report all three factors, 38% two factors, and 18% one factor. Only 3% of nascent entrepreneurs have none of these positive features.

Knowing that these three factors have a major impact on readiness for entrepreneurship leads to an interest in their causes. For example, an interest in or capacity to identify business opportunities is probably facilitated by being embedded in a social network of business owners. They will be exposed to dinner table stories about identifying business opportunities and the procedures required to take advantage of them. Greater sensitivity to economic opportunities may also be enhanced in a cultural setting that values business creation or working in sectors where there is a constant turnover of business firms, such as residential construction or restaurants. Such contexts and experiences may lead individuals to be more alert to potential business opportunities.

Confidence in having the skill or ability to implement a firm may reflect two types of experiences. First, one could work for a new or small business, observing how the owner–managers develop and manage a new venture. This could be in the context of a family business or early career employment. Second, one could take formal coursework on business creation, the core element of most educational programs on entrepreneurship. Either of these experiences may lead to social networks that include others involved in business creation and a greater personal emphasis on identifying business opportunities.

For example, those that grow up in a setting where friends and relatives are involved in business creation or small business ownership are much more likely to consider this a viable career option. Just as those that are raised in communities where everybody works in large companies or for government agencies are more likely to consider wage work the most appropriate career path.

Those that see business opportunities, are confident they have the skill to implement a new firm, and have personal social networks that include other business creators are more likely to pursue business creation. This suggests those interested in an entrepreneurial career may benefit from pursuing these attributes—exploring business opportunities, developing the skills for business administration, and pursuing social contacts with entrepreneurs.

PERSONAL CHARACTERISTICS AND PARTICIPATION[10]

If there are 16.3 million people involved in business creation, what does this mass of entrepreneurs look like? They can be described in terms of their socio-demographic background, the human capital they have acquired, and their financial context.

As shown in Table 3.1, the largest single group are men 35–44 years old; this is about 3.4 million individuals that are 21% of all active nascent entrepreneurs. The next largest group are the 2.4 million women of the same age, 35–44 years old, who are 15% of the total. There are about 1.6 million very young adults, those 18 to 24 years old; they are slightly less than 10% of the total. Seniors, those 65 and over, account for about 2% of the total, but number about 300,000 of the total. Business creation is clearly a mid-career effort, as four in five (79%) are between 25 and 54 years old, accounting for 13 million nascent entrepreneurs.

Because they are the majority of the population, Whites account for 11 million nascent entrepreneurs, 68% of the total. The next largest group are African-Americans; these 2.9 million nascent entrepreneurs are 18% of the total. Hispanic Americans are about 5% of the total, accounting for almost a million. The heterogeneous other category provides about 1.5 million, or 9%.

Immigrant business creation gets a lot of attention, especially those involved with high technology ventures. While there is no question that immigrants may be more likely to pursue firm creation and many highly skilled immigrants come to the U.S. for work, in high technology businesses, the image of U.S. business creation dominated by immigrants is slightly misleading. In cohorts representing the entire U.S. population of nascent entrepreneurs[11] about one in 25 (4%) are individuals born outside the U.S. of parents born outside the U.S. Another 1% are born outside the U.S. with one parent born in the U.S. Another 8% are U.S. born but at least one parent was born outside the U.S. While immigrants in the United States may be more likely to pursue business creation, as of 1999 and 2005 19 in 20 (96%) of those involved are native born; they are 15.5 million of the nascent entrepreneurs. About a million nascent entrepreneurs were born outside the United States; they are 5% of the total.

Recent internal migrants are a small part of the nascent entrepreneur population. Slightly more than one million have lived in

Table 3.1   Participation in business creation and socio-demographic
            characteristics[12]

	Proportion Nascent Entrepreneurs (%)	Total number
Men by Age		
18–24 Years old	6.6	1,100,000
25–34 Years old	14.3	2,300,000
35–44 Years old	20.6	3,400,000
45–54 Years old	11.2	1,800,000
55–64 Years old	4.7	800,000
65 up Years old	1.4	200,000
Women by Age		
18–24 Years old	2.8	500,000
25–34 Years old	11.7	1,900,000
35–44 Years old	14.6	2,400,000
45–54 Years old	6.9	1,100,000
55–64 Years old	4.7	800,000
65 up Years old	0.6	100,000
	100.0	
Ethnic background		
White	67.9	11,100,000
African-American	17.7	2,900,000
Hispanic American	5.3	900,000
Mixed/Other	9.1	1,500,000
	100.0	
U.S. immigration		
Entrepreneur U.S. born	94.7	15,500,000
Entrepreneur born outside U.S.	5.3	900,000
	100.0	
County immigrant, lived		
Up to 1 year	6.9	1,100,000
2–9 years	35.1	5,700,000
10–29 years	35.8	5,800,000
30+ years	22.2	3,600,000
	100.0	

their county for less than a year. Seven in ten (71%) have lived in the county for two to 29 years; they are 11.5 million of the business creators. Those resident over 30 years are a major source, one in five, of nascent entrepreneurs. This suggests that those involved in business creation need some time to get accustomed to their new context.

The human capital of those active in business creation is summarized in Table 3.2. Those from all educational backgrounds are well represented in the population of nascent entrepreneurs, although those with post-high school community college, vocational, or tech-

Table 3.2   Participation in business creation and human capital[13]

	Proportion Nascent Entrepreneurs (%)	Total Number
Educational Attainment		
Up to high school degree	21.9	3,600,000
Post-high school, pre-college	37.0	6,000,000
College degree	24.8	4,000,000
Graduate experience	16.4	2,700,000
	100.1	
Work status at entry		
Full-time work for others	45.2	7,400,000
Part-time work for others	17.1	2,800,000
Business owner, self-employed	22.3	3,600,000
Homemaker	9.1	1,500,000
Unemployed	4.9	800,000
Student/retired/disabled	1.4	200,000
	100.0	
Same Sector Work Experience		
None	29.0	4,800,000
1–5 years	27.4	4,500,000
6–14 years	20.3	3,300,000
15+ years	23.3	3,800,000
	100.0	
Other Start-up Experiences		
None	57.5	9,400,000
One other	22.3	3,600,000
Two+	20.2	3,300,000
	100.0	

nical training but without college degrees are the largest single group. These six million are 37% of the total.

Most significant is the work status as nascent entrepreneurs enter the start-up process. Over four in five (85%) are involved with work of some kind as they pursue business creation. They are almost 14 million of the nascent entrepreneurs. Those not involved in work, particularly homemakers and the unemployed, are a small proportion (15%) of the total, accounting for about 2.5 million nascent entrepreneurs.

Most, over 70%, involved have work experience in the sector where they are pursuing business creation. A substantial minority, 44%, have six or more years of same sector work experience, accounting for over seven million of active nascent entrepreneurs. On the other hand, three in five (58%) have no previous experience with business creation. Almost 10 million are first time nascent entrepreneurs. The 3.3 million working on their third start-up are one-fifth of the total.

The personal financial situation, represented by the annual household income and net worth of the nascent entrepreneur is presented in Table 3.3. By both measures, nascent entrepreneurs come from a wide range of contexts. All annual income and network categories are represented in the population of nascent entrepreneurs. Of some interest is the representation among those from very modest contexts: those with annual household income below $20,000 are almost one in ten (9%), accounting for 1.4 million individuals. Those with either negative or no net worth are one in eight (13%) and account for two million nascent entrepreneurs. Those at the other extreme, annual incomes of $100,000 or more and household net worth greater than half a million ($500,000), are also a significant portion of the nascent entrepreneur population.

But three in four of those participating are, by either measure, from the middle of the distribution, accounting for 12 million of the population of nascent entrepreneurs.

Substantial numbers of individuals with a wide range of socio-demographic backgrounds, with very diverse human capital, and all financial contexts are involved in business creation.

OVERVIEW

Business creation is a very popular career option, pursued by millions. But some rather stable patterns are found in the United States.

Table 3.3   *Participation in business creation and personal financial context*[14]

	Proportion Nascent Entrepreneurs (%)	Total Number
Household Income (before taxes, $2005)		
Up to $20,000/year	8.8	1,400,000
$20,001 to $40,000/year	21.0	3,400,000
$40,001 to $60,000/year	23.4	3,800,000
$60,001 to $80,000/year	15.3	2,500,000
$80,001 to $100,000/year	14.3	2,300,000
$100,001 to $150,000/year	11.2	1,800,000
$150,001 and higher/year	6.2	1,000,000
	100.2	
Household Net Worth ($2005)		
Negative, up to $0	12.7	2,100,000
$1 to $25,000	13.9	2,300,000
$25,001 to $100,000	30.0	4,900,000
$100,001 to $200,000	16.8	2,700,000
$200,001 to $500,000	15.4	2,500,000
$500,001 to $1,000,000	6.3	1,000,000
$1,000,001 and higher	4.5	900,000
	99.6	

- Every group or category of people are involved in business creation.
- There is lots of activity in the pre-profit or start-up stage.
- Ethnic minorities are more active compared to the White majority; but the majority of active nascent entrepreneurs are White.
- Nineteen in 20 of U.S. nascent entrepreneurs are native born.
- Readiness for entrepreneurship leads to much higher participation in business creation.
- Those from all socio-demographic categories complete the process with profitable new firms.

But while it is relatively straightforward to predict the tendency of individuals to pursue business creation, there are always exceptions and plenty of examples of individuals that "break all the rules." Ashok Khade started from the untouchable caste in rural India in 1955 to found a $100 million construction company specializing in offshore drilling rigs with 4,500 employees.[15]

POLICY IMPLICATIONS

There is no social category of citizens that are not involved in business creation. Many factors affecting participation—age, gender, ethnic background—are not easily affected by public policy. There might be programs tailored to groups where more participation is seen as desirable—such as women or older adults.

Facilitating personal readiness for entrepreneurship, which reflects being embedded in social networks of business creators, perception of business opportunities, and confidence in business creation skills, may increase active participation in entrepreneurial initiatives. Of these, the one most amenable to policy influence is development of business creation skills. Including training business creation in educational programs at all levels would present entrepreneurship as a legitimate career option, which could also lead to more nascent ventures.

NOTES

1. Prevalence rates are the average values for 2005 to 2014, except for 2010, from the Global Entrepreneurship Monitor consolidated data base (Reynolds and Hechavarria, 2016). This project uses the same conceptual definition of nascent entrepreneurs, with a slightly different operational definition. Population estimates based on U.S. Census Population by Age and Sex estimates for 2010 (U.S. Census, U.S. Department of Commerce, no date).
2. PSED SAMPID 51609, fictitious names.
3. PSED SAMPID 1596, fictitious names.
4. PSED SAMPID 51665, fictitious names.
5. Based on Reynolds and Curtin (2009a), Figure 7.4 and U.S. Census Estimates of Population by Race, Sex, and Hispanic origin for July 2009 (U.S. Census, U.S. Department of Commerce, no date). Hispanic count includes all self-identified Hispanics.
6. Those with an ethnic identity of "Other," including Asians, American Indians, and Pacific Islanders, account for 300,000 nascent entrepreneurs.
7. PSED SAMPID 8090, fictitious names.
8. PSED SAMPID 1607, fictitious names.
9. Based on 29,134 cases in representative samples of the U.S. adult population

developed from the year 2000 to 2012 as part of the Global Entrepreneurship Monitor program (Reynolds, 2015).

10. The following discussion is based on a sample of nascent entrepreneurs with weights adjusted to compensate for duration in the start-up process. The data set that is the source of Figures 3.1 and 3.2 does not have the information to provide this adjustment. As a result, there may be some variation in the two descriptions.

11. Summaries of cohorts of nascent entrepreneurs are summarized in Table 3.1, after case weights adjusted for biases in sampling, start-up team size, and duration in the start-up process.

12. All characteristics are harmonized across both U.S. PSED I and II data sets, and include only cases with data on 72 month outcomes (n=1,418). Case weights adjusted for biases in sample screening, start-up team size, and duration in the start-up process. Respondents were allowed to select multiple labor force relationships, that is, they could be both disabled and a homemaker. A single labor force participation was selected for each case in the order presented in Table 3.1.

13. All values are in 2005 U.S. dollars, 1999 values adjusted using the Consumer Price Index (CPI). Case weights adjusted to compensate for biases in sample screening, start-up team size, and duration in the start-up process. Household assessment based on 1,311 cases and net worth assessment based on 1,131 cases.

14. All values are in 2005 U.S. dollars; 1999 values adjusted using the Consumer Price Index (CPI). Case weights adjusted to compensate for biases in sample screening, start-up team size, and duration in the start-up process. Household assessment based on 1,311 cases and net worth assessment based on 1,131 cases.

15. Polgreen (2011).

4. Motives are diverse and may change

The corporate world has been very restrictive so Barbara wants to develop her own practice as a career and executive coach. She likes helping people achieve their goals on a personal level. She can be more helpful if she can coordinate all her skills and methodologies. Barbara just completed an MA and gets a lot of positive feedback from those she helped. With a network of experienced colleagues there is access to a lot of expertise for difficult issues.[1]

George says he is too old to start a retirement plan and doesn't want to be in a dark corner eating cat food and peeing on himself when he is 70. With several patents, including one for processing digital audio tapes that is unique and useful for those replacing VHS tapes, he sees a competitive advantage. George is starting Smith-Rogers Audio Productions to develop and market this hardware and promote musical talent.[2]

Lynn worked in home design and lived in the same community for 20 years. She realizes that the community is becoming more affluent and there are more customers for unique home decorations. Working with other designers, Affordable Interiors will utilize Lynn's contacts in Mexico to create custom-made wrought iron pieces and provide distinctive treatments at competitive prices.[3]

Roger didn't like taking orders from someone who didn't know what they were doing and making money from his work. He says his team is damn good at what they do and can be successful with consulting clients on information processing without sponsorship from a corporate giant.[4]

Nascent entrepreneurs have a range of motives for getting involved in business creation. A summary of primary motives is provided in Table 4.1. These vary from a desire to work on a new idea of their own, mentioned by 23%, to hoping to make a social or economic contribution, mentioned by 2%. Those motives most widely discussed—such as financial gain (20%), work autonomy (19%), and pursuit of an opportunity (19%)—are represented but none is dominant. On the other hand, the top four—particularly financial gain—are frequently mentioned as a secondary reason for

Table 4.1   Reasons for pursuing business creation[5]

	First Response (%)	Second Response (%)
Pursue new idea, work on own topics	23.1	18.7
Financial gain	19.7	26.0
Flexibility and autonomy at work	19.2	18.1
Pursue business opportunity	19.1	11.7
Personal, family, or lifestyle issues	11.6	8.2
Best option for having work	5.5	7.1
Make a social or economic contribution	1.8	10.2
Total	100.0	100.0

getting involved in business creation, evidence that many have mixed motives. No one reason is dominant; most entrepreneurs report a mix of motivations.

Scholarly efforts to explore entrepreneurial motivation have focused on a number of issues. Is business creation a response to the economic context, with some pulled into entrepreneurship by an attractive business opportunity, or are business creators "cast off from wage work"[6] and pushed into entrepreneurship? Are there intrinsic rewards of business ownership that attract people to business creation? Are entrepreneurs driven by some inner psychic need from birth, reflected in an entrepreneurial personality? Do those involved in business creation have distinctive preferences, like a need for achievement or a preference for risk? All these individual features may differentiate those in business creation from typical adults and may be related to the outcome of the business creation process. The following reviews a selection of motivations and personal characteristics associated with participation in business creation and the outcomes.

CONTEXTUAL MOTIVATION

The four examples at the beginning, reflecting the comments of Barbara, George, Lynn, and Roger, were individuals pursuing business opportunities. But others get involved in response to their personal context:

My government agency was downsized and I was let go so I needed to find work.[7]

I wanted to get out of the factory.[8]

I got tired of looking for a job.[9]

To be my own independent person and let my creative side come out.[10]

I am handicapped, don't drive, taught myself HTML and now have programming customers. My resumé, however, is still in circulation.'[11]

These individuals are pursuing business creation because it is, from their perspective, their best option in response to the local economy and their personal situation. If circumstances changed, they could well pursue different career options. Furthermore, if their new venture is successful, they may find business ownership a better option than working for others.

This is often referred to as the "push" from lack of work options rather than the "pull" of attractive business opportunities. When U.S. nascent entrepreneurs are asked about whether they are attracted to an opportunity or responding to limited options for work, Table 4.2 indicates that almost nine in ten (87%) indicate they are responding to opportunities. About one in ten (10%) say the lack of good options is the major factor. Another one in 33 (3%) say it is a combination of both.

There is little difference among men and women or nascent

Table 4.2   Contextual motivations and participation in business creation[12]

	All Nascent Entrepreneurs (%)	Growth Oriented Nascent Entrepreneurs (%)	Easy to Manage Business Creators (%)	Statistical Significance
Opportunity	87.3	91.8	85.7	
Combination	2.7	1.9	3.0	
No better choice	10.0	6.3	11.3	ns
	100.0	100.0	100.0	

Note: Statistical significance: ns = not significant at 0.05.

entrepreneurs of different ages in their response to the context. Those working while they pursue business creation are slightly more likely to be responding to opportunity. Two in five of those not working, such as the unemployed, disabled, or retired, are more likely to mention that business creation is their best choice. Still, three in-five of those not working mention the attraction of a business opportunity.

Many consider that real entrepreneurs are interested in high growth ventures. Among those involved in business creation, this can be determined by asking about their aspirations for the new firm. When asked, about one in four (23%) involved in business creation seek to maximize the growth of their nascent venture; three in four (77%) seek a business that is easy to manage.[13] There is, as shown in Table 4.2, a modest association between pursuing a business opportunity and interest in a growth venture, but the difference is not statistically significant.

CONTEXTUAL MOTIVATION: CROSS-NATIONAL COMPARISONS

Some of the most dramatic differences in business creation occur across different countries. There is substantial variation in both the level of participation as well as reports of contextual motivation. These are presented in Figure 4.1, which compares the patterns for eight global regions: North America, Oceania (Australia, Canada, New Zealand, and the United States); Western Europe; Developed Asia (Japan, Taiwan, Singapore, and South Korea); Middle East, North Africa; Developing Asia (China, India, and others); Central and Eastern Europe; Sub-Sahara Africa; and Latin America and the Caribbean.[14] Countries in each region are weighted to reflect the proportion of adults 18–64 years old. As a result, the United States has a much bigger impact on the North America, Oceania prevalence rate than Australia, Canada, or New Zealand.

The height of the bars represents the prevalence of nascent entrepreneurs, which varies from four to 16 per 100 adults 18–64 years in age. The different shades represent differential responses to the context: opportunity, best choice, or a mixture of both. The eight regions are organized, from left to right, in terms of the level of participation in business creation. But this is also a rough measure of economic development, with three regions with the poorest countries to the far right. Three regions with the most developed countries are to the left.

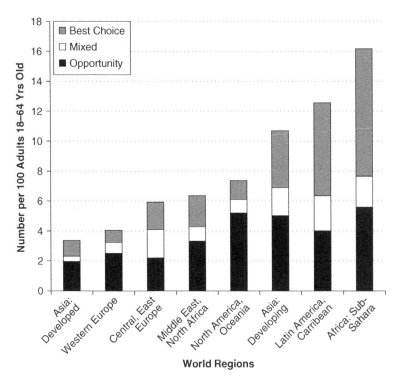

Figure 4.1   Participation in business creation by contextual motivation: world regions

There are two exceptions. First, the four Anglo countries in North America and Oceania with similar political histories have levels of participation somewhat higher than other developed countries, particularly Western Europe. Second, the Middle East, North Africa region has less business creation than North America, Oceania. This reflects the low participation of women in the economics of these countries with a high proportion of Muslims. There is, to be sure, much variation among the Islamic countries.[15]

Perhaps the most important pattern is that the level of participation is generally much higher in developing countries where the economies are more diverse and there are fewer wage and salary jobs. And a large proportion of these jobs are in government agencies. This is robust evidence that the economic and social context have a major impact on participation in business creation.

In addition, the contextual motivation varies dramatically. Those with no better options are a much higher proportion of business creators in developing countries. Participation due to a lack of good options varies from about one per 100 in Western Europe and Developed Asian regions to eight per 100 in Sub-Sahara Africa. Participation to pursue opportunities varies from two per 100 in the Developed Asian countries to more than five per 100 in North America, Oceania; Developing Asia; and Sub-Sahara Africa. For both forms of contextual motivation, the context has a major effect on the amount of participation.

This global assessment makes clear that the state of the national economy, level of development, and the presence of established public and private work organizations may affect the context in which individuals pursue business creation. Similar differences can be found among the regions within large, diverse countries.

INTRINSIC REWARDS

Entrepreneurs seek four types of intrinsic rewards from launching a successful enterprise.

● Autonomy: reflecting the desire for freedom and developing a flexible relationship between work, family, and personal life.[16]
● Wealth or the importance of a larger personal income: financial security, and greater wealth.[17]
● Task achievement: an emphasis on development of new business ideas, fulfilling a personal vision, improving personal status and recognition, or the ability to influence an organization.[18]
● Respect: the desire to follow a family tradition, emulate an admired mentor, gain respect from friends, or creating a business for one's children.[19]

Virtually all those involved report a mixture of these emphases; rarely is one the sole reason for participation in business creation. The relative emphasis on these four motivations are presented Figure 4.2. All nascent entrepreneurs are represented by the black bar, growth oriented nascents by the grey bar, and typical adults by the white bars.

All intrinsic motivations are important. The highest average

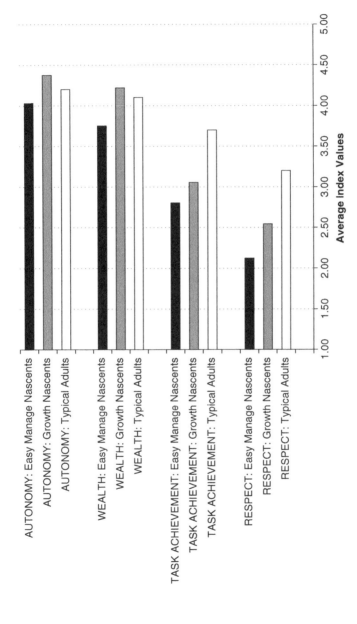

Figure 4.2   Intrinsic motivation of nascent entrepreneurs

31

value "of great importance"or 4.0 is associated with autonomy. The emphasis on wealth is slightly below but higher than of "some importance". The emphasis on task achievement and respect are both between "of little" and "some" importance. None has an average value of 1.0, representing "no importance."

When nascent entrepreneurs are compared by gender, age, and labor force status the rank order across the four intrinsic motivations is remarkably consistent, in the order of autonomy, wealth, task achievement, and respect (from others). Women, older, and retired nascent entrepreneurs may give less significance to intrinsic motivations, but these differences are small. The preferences of those unemployed and disabled appear to be almost identical to those working while starting a business.

Nascent entrepreneurs are, apparently, very similar to typical adults regarding an interest in autonomy or wealth. They are less concerned with task achievement or gathering respect from others than typical adults. Growth oriented nascent entrepreneurs appear to be more like typical adults than those planning for an easy to manage business.

Those involved in business creation seem to be attracted to the same intrinsic motivations as all adults. They have, however, chosen a different path for fulfilment.

IS ENTREPRENEURSHIP GENETIC?

If all entrepreneurs reflect a genetic predisposition, then one would expect the majority of those involved in business creation to say they are seeking a suitable business opportunity to satisfy a motivation to be a business owner. When those active in business creation are asked about the process of becoming involved, about three in ten report that the desire to create a business led to the search or development of a business opportunities.[20] A slightly greater proportion, about four in ten, report that discovery or identification of a business opportunity occurred first. This was followed by a realization that they would need to create a business to take advantage of the opportunity. The remainder, about one-third, say that the two events—recognizing a business opportunity and desire to be an entrepreneur—occurred at the same time.

It is reasonable to assume that both mechanisms are present, leading different individuals to become active in business creation for different reasons. Some are born to be an entrepreneur and others discover that entrepreneurship is attractive.

Personal Dispositions

Those responsible for new businesses often seem highly focused, driven, rather self-centered, and considered to have a high need for achievement. This has led many to search for a personal trait or characteristic that will identify those that were born to be an entrepreneur or achieve self-fulfillment as their own boss.

The impact of seven personal dispositions is explored by considering two comparisons. First, the differences between nascent entrepreneurs and typical workers, both identified at the same time in a representative sample of adults. Second, the difference between two types of nascent entrepreneurs, those that wish to maximize the growth of their new venture and those that wish to have a business that is easy to manage. Growth oriented entrepreneurs are often considered "real entrepreneurs."

Need for Achievement

Those with a high need for achievement (N-Ach) are considered to work with a singleness of purpose toward a high and distant goal and to have a determination to win.[21] Many consider it a central feature of "real entrepreneurs." A six-item measure of this construct was developed by a team of scholars for the PSED I assessment to include the following items.[22]

- I would quit a job because it was not challenging.
- I would like to be better at things I try.
- I would like to have people pay attention to what I have to say.
- If doing well on an important project, I would consider the work yet to be done.
- I can do anything I set my mind on doing.
- I spend time making organizations I belong to function better.

As most were dichotomous, the scale consisted of adding up the total number of "N-Ach responses." The scale had a range of 0 to 6 and was recoded into low, medium and high values to facilitate comparisons.[23]

As can be seen in Table 4.3, those active in business creation were

Table 4.3 Need for achievement and participation in business creation[24]

	Typical Adults (%)	Nascent Entrepreneurs (%)	Statistical Significance	Easy to Manage Nascent Entrepreneurs (%)	Growth Oriented Nascent Entrepreneurs (%)	Statistical Significance
Need for Achievement						
High	23.8	30.3		31.0	32.6	
Medium	37.5	42.1		42.9	39.5	
Low	38.7	27.6		26.1	27.9	
	100.0	100.0	**	100.0	100.0	ns

Note: Statistical significance: ns = not significant at 0.05; **=0.01.

slightly higher on need for achievement than the typical adults, but the difference is just barely statistically significant. However, there is no substantive difference between growth oriented nascent entrepreneurs and those seeking an easy to manage venture.

Risk Preference

One of the more enduring proposals regarding business creation is that it attracts those with a preference for risk. Many consider entrepreneurs as those willing to gamble with their careers—and their life savings. Two comparisons of preference for risk are available.

One comparison is of nascent entrepreneurs and typical adults asked for their preference between two businesses:

- Sleepwell: A business that would provide a good living, but with little risk of failure, and little likelihood of making you a millionaire.
- Eatwell: A business that was much more likely to make you a millionaire but had a much higher chance of going bankrupt.

The Sleepwell option would lead to less financial return but less worry about losses, and the Eatwell choice would be associated with greater financial rewards but more concern about its stability.[25]

As presented in Table 4.4, the proportion of those involved in business creation that chose Eatwell, the higher risk and higher return option, is only slightly higher than typical adults. The difference is not statistically significant. But the high growth nascent entrepreneurs are over twice as likely to choose the Eatwell option as typical adults and three times as likely as the easy to manage firm. A difference that is highly statistically significant.

A second comparison, profit versus risk, asks individuals to choose between one of three options. Each has the same "expected value" of $1 million but with different probabilities.[26]

- Profit of $5,000,000, with a 20% chance of success.
- Profit of $2,000,000, with a 50% chance of success.
- Profit of $1,250,000, with an 80% chance of success.

Those with a preference or tolerance for risk would be expected to choose the first option.

Table 4.4 Risk orientation and participation in business creation[27]

	Typical Adults (%)	Nascent Entrepreneurs (%)	Statistical Significance	Easy to Manage Nascent Entrepreneurs (%)	Growth Oriented Nascent Entrepreneurs (%)	Statistical Significance
Risk Preference						
Eatwell (Seek returns)	15.0	16.4		11.0	36.0	
Sleepwell (Avoid risk)	85.0	83.6	ns	89.0	64.0	***
	100.0	100.0		100.0	100.0	
Profit vs Risk						
20% chance of $5,000,000	11.8	11.9		9.6	20.0	
50% chance of $2,000,000	26.1	26.5		26.2	25.9	
80% chance of $1,250,000	62.8	61.6	ns	64.2	54.1	*
	100.0	100.0		100.1	100.0	

Note: Statistical significance: ns=not significant; *=0.05; ***=0.001.

The actual preferences, comparing representative samples of those involved in business creation with those not involved is presented in Table 4.4. As with the first measure of risk preference, there is no substantively or statistically significant difference between those involved in business creation and the typical adults. Growth oriented nascent entrepreneurs are, however, more likely to choose the higher risk outcomes when compared to the easy to manage business creators.

RISK PREFERENCE COMMENTARY

In both comparisons related to risk preferences the results are the same. First, when compared to typical adults, those involved in business creation are just as likely to choose the two low risk options, Sleepwell rather than Eatwell, and a preference for a sure thing, the modest payout of $1,250,000.

But there is some diversity among those involved in business creation. When those that claim they seek the highest possible growth are compared to those that hope for a business that is comfortable to manage, more growth oriented nascent entrepreneurs select the higher risk, higher payoff options. Even so, the majority of growth oriented nascent entrepreneurs chose the low risk options. Two-thirds (64%) chose the Sleepwell business and over half (54%) chose the sure thing, an 80% chance at $1,250,000.

This conservative posture is consistent with the contextual situation of those active in business creation, reflected in Tables 3.1 and 3.2. The majority, four of five, are working or managing a business while they are developing a new venture. Seven in ten have one or more years of work experience in the same industry and about half have six or more years of experience. Further, over 90% are starting a business where they have lived for some time, 60% have lived in the same county for ten or more years. Most prefer a context where their spouse may have established a career (with retirement and health care benefits). Once well established in a community, nascent entrepreneurs will know something of the customers, competitors, and suppliers; they are able to locate partners, employees, and formal and informal financial support; and will know where they can locate work if the new start-up is not successful.

This is not an image of individuals driven to risk time and money in the pursuit of riches. While bankers and professors may consider entrepreneurs as pursuing risk, those starting new businesses consider the effort low risk or with manageable risks that are justified by the payoffs.

Business creators are not reckless gamblers.[28]

ENTREPRENEURIAL INTENSITY

Some involved in business creation are more committed than others. Entrepreneurial intensity is considered the level of commitment to and focus on business creation.[29] A four-item index to measure entrepreneurial intensity is based on the following items:

- My personal philosophy is to do "whatever it takes" to establish my own business.
- Would rather own my own business than earn a higher salary employed by someone else.
- Owning my own business is more important than spending time with my family.
- There is no limit as to how long I would give maximum effort to establish my business.

Responses are obtained on a five-point scale, from "completely true" to "completely untrue." The average value of the responses to the four items provides a measure of entrepreneurial intensity, or the extent to which the respondent is committed to this career option.[30] This measure is then reorganized into three categories: high, medium and low levels of entrepreneurial intensity. Comparisons are presented in Table 4.5.

Over one-third of those involved in business creation have a high level of entrepreneurial intensity at the beginning of the process; almost half of the typical adults have a low level of intensity. The difference is highly statistically significant. The differences among nascent entrepreneurs with different aspirations is more nuanced. Over two-in-five easy to manage business creators reflect low levels of intensity, while almost three fourths of growth oriented nascent entrepreneurs have medium or high levels of intensity. Both differences are highly statistically significant.

Table 4.5   Entrepreneurial intensity and participation in business creation[31]

	Typical Adults (%)	Nascent Entrepreneurs (%)	Statistical Significance	Easy to Manage Nascent Entrepreneurs (%)	Growth Oriented Nascent Entrepreneurs (%)	Statistical Significance
Entrepreneurial Intensity						
High	18.7	37.1		39.0	28.7	
Medium	16.0	23.4		18.3	42.5	
Low	65.3	39.5	***	42.7	28.7	***
	100.0	100.0		100.0	99.9	

Note: Statistical significance: ns = not significant; ***=0.001.

PERSONAL CONTROL OF OUTCOMES

People vary in terms of their beliefs about factors affecting outcomes. Some consider major events are affect by external factors, which they cannot influence. Others feel confident they can personally affect outcomes. Many efforts to identify perceptions of the locus of control have been developed.[32] In this assessment, three items were utilized to create a locus of control index:

- I have no trouble making and keeping friends.
- When I make plans I am almost certain to make them work.
- When I get what I want, it is usually because I worked hard for it.

Responses were provided on a five-point scale from "completely untrue" to "completely true" and the average value defined the index.[33]

As shown in Table 4.6, there is no difference between all business creators and typical adults in the perception they can control important outcomes. Those growth oriented nascent entrepreneurs do have a statistically significant greater confidence in their ability to control outcomes compared to easy to manage business creators.

Innovation versus Adaptation

Business creation involves developing new systems and procedures, often to produce new products and services. When confronted with a challenge, some individuals make efforts to improve and refine existing procedures, and are considered to be adaptors. Others, considered to be innovators, tend to develop new systems, procedures, or products to replace those that are established. Depending on the nature of the new business, and the associated problems, either strategy may have success.[34]

Based on a review of substantial efforts to identify decision-making styles, the following items were utilized to determine whether individuals emphasized adaptation or innovation.

- If someone asked you which kind of person you are, would you say that you preferred "doing things better" or "doing things differently?"

Table 4.6 Personal dispositions and participation in business creation[35]

	Typical Adults	Nascent Entrepreneurs	Statistical Significance	Easy to Manage Nascent Entrepreneurs	Growth Oriented Nascent Entrepreneurs	Statistical Significance
Personal Control of Outcomes	4.0	4.0	ns	3.9	4.3	***
Adaptive/Innovative Decisions	1.4	1.6	***	1.7	1.4	***
Economic Sophistication	3.2	3.2	ns	3.2	3.2	ns

Note: Statistical significance: ns = not significant; *** =0.001.

- How well does your preferred style of problem-solving match the types of problems encountered in starting a new business? Would you say your style is often a good match, sometimes a good match, sometimes a poor match, or often a poor match?
- Consider your closest associate helping you start this business. Would you consider this a person who preferred "doing things better" or "doing things differently?"

The average value was used to create an index, which would be higher for those that emphasized innovation and lower for those that emphasized adaptation.[36]

As shown in Table 4.6, those involved in business creation are more likely to emphasize innovation, and compared to typical adults, the difference is statistically significant. In contrast, growth oriented entrepreneurs tended to emphasize adaptation, compared with easy to manage business creators, which is also statistically significant.

Economic Sophistication

Implementing a new business involves, if nothing else, decisions about the allocation of economic resources.[37] Those that are more sophisticated about economic decision making may be more confident regarding their ability to implement a new firm. Two items were used to create a measure of economic sophistication.

- If I am about to leave home for a game or concert and discover I have lost the ticket, I will buy another ticket and go anyway.
- When I decide whether to keep or sell an investment, I consider the investment's current value rather than what I paid for it.

In both cases, responses were on a five-point scale, from "completely untrue" to "completely true." Presumably, one sophisticated in economic decision making would answer "completely true" to both items. In both cases, the lost ticket and purchase of the investment are "sunk costs," which should be ignored in relation to future benefits—attending the concert or sale of the investment.

The average value was used as an indicator of economic sophistication; a higher value would reflect greater sophistication.[38] As can be seen in the third row of Table 4.6, there is no statistically significant difference between typical adults, all business creators, or growth oriented nascent entrepreneurs. The average value for all three groups is slightly greater than "it depends," or "slightly true."

Motives and Orientations Overview

In terms of intrinsic motivations, nascent entrepreneurs are similar to typical adults with regards an interest in autonomy or wealth, and typical adults reflect a greater interest in task achievement and developing respect. Comparing typical adults with active nascent entrepreneurs on six orientations finds three with significant differences. Nascent entrepreneurs tend to reflect a high need for achievement, a high level of entrepreneurial intensity, and a preference for innovative decision making when confronted with a complication. There was no significant difference related to preferences for risk, confidence in the ability to control outcomes, or economic sophistication.

Those nascents responding to business opportunities were slightly more likely to be interested in a growth venture, but the difference was not statistically significant. Growth oriented nascents did have a greater focus on all four intrinsic motivations—autonomy, greater wealth, a task focus, and developing respect—when compared to easy to manage business creators. There were also differences on four orientations between nascent entrepreneurs seeking to have a growth business and business creators seeking an easy to manage venture. Growth oriented nascents reflected a higher preference for higher payoff, greater risk options; greater intensity of commitment; were more likely to consider they could control outcomes; and had an adaptive decision-making orientation. There was no difference related to a need for achievement or economic sophistication. Overall, growth oriented nascents were more consistent with the popular image of entrepreneurs.

Most differences, even those highly statistically significant, did not reflect major substantive differences. In fact, it is clear that there is considerable diversity among those in all three groups, typical adults, growth oriented nascent entrepreneurs, and easy to manage firm creators. Personality traits may not be very useful in predicting who will enter into business creation or emphasize a growth business strategy.[39] It has been suggested that who is an entrepreneur is the wrong question; it may be more useful to ask how entrepreneurship occurs.[40] Considering the relationship between these orientations and the outcomes of participating in business creation helps to determine their predictive usefulness.

MOTIVES, DISPOSITIONS, AND OUTCOMES

It is possible that the motives and orientations of nascent entrepreneurs may affect the outcome. Thirteen comparisons are presented in Table 4.7. In every case the measures of orientation occurred early in the process, during the first detailed interviews, and outcomes were tracked over the following years. There are statistically significant differences for six comparisons; no relationship to outcomes for seven; and many of the relationships are unexpected.

Perhaps the strongest pattern in the expected direction is the low proportion of those with a low Need for Achievement that report initial profitability: 28% compared to 53% with an intermediate level and 39% with the higher Need for Achievement index score.

In contrast, the measure of Entrepreneurial Intensity, which is also related to outcomes, indicates that a larger proportion of those with a low measure are more likely to reach initial profitability (52%), compared to those with a medium (27%) or high (39%) level of intensity. The high and medium intensity nascents are also more likely to have disengaged. As nascents with lower levels of intensity were more likely to be interested in an easy to manage business, they may be working on less complicated initiatives that are easier to implement.

There is a statistically significant relation to outcomes for all four intrinsic motivations—autonomy, wealth, task focus, and respect. But the major association is the lower values associated with those that quit, compared to those still active or having achieved profitability. While statistically significant, the differences are modest.

Several orientations are suggestive, though not statistically significant. Those that report a focus on growth are also more likely to reach initial profitability, compared to those seeking an easy to manage business (41% versus 36%). They are equally likely to have disengaged (47% and 48%). Those that consider business creation their best choice for work are less likely to report initial profitability than those pursuing business opportunities (26% versus 34%) and more likely to have disengaged (65% versus 53%), but the difference is not statistically significant. This may reflect the small number of individuals pursuing their best choice.

Table 4.7 Motivations, dispositions and outcomes[41]

	Initial Profitability	Active Start-up	Quit	Row Totals (%)	Statistical Significance
Growth Orientation					
Maximize Growth	41.4%	12.0%	46.6%	100.0	
Easy to Manage	36.5%	15.6%	47.9%	100.1	ns
Contextual Motivation					
Opportunity	34.1%	12.8%	53.0%	99.9	
Combination	39.1%	8.7%	52.2%	100.0	
No better choice	25.9%	8.6%	65.4%	100.0	ns
Intrinsic Motivation (Averages)					
Autonomy	3.9	4.2	3.9		**
Wealth	3.6	3.9	3.5		***
Task focus, recognition	2.6	3.0	2.6		***
Respect	2.1	2.4	2.1		***
Need for Achievement					
High	38.7%	16.0%	45.4%	100.1	
Medium	52.7%	14.4%	32.9%	100.0	
Low	27.5%	30.3%	42.2%	100.0	***

Table 4.7 (continued)

	Initial Profitability	Active Start-up	Quit	Row Totals (%)	Statistical Significance
Entrepreneurial Intensity					
High	39.2%	18.2%	42.6%	100.0	
Medium	27.2%	27.2%	45.7%	100.1	
Low	51.9%	15.8%	32.3%	100.0	**
Risk Preference					
Eatwell (Seek returns)	35.4%	24.6%	40.0%	100.0	
Sleepwell (Avoid risk)	42.6%	18.3%	39.0%	100.0	ns
Profit vs Risk					
20% chance of $5,000,000	39.1%	13.0%	47.8%	100.0	
50% chance of $2,000,000	46.7%	12.4%	41.0%	100.0	
80% chance of $1,250,000	40.3%	23.5%	36.2%	100.0	ns
Personal Control of Outcomes	4.0	4.0	4.0		ns
Innovative/Adaptive Decisions	1.7	1.6	1.6		ns
Economic Sophistication	3.2	3.3	3.1		ns

Note: Statistical significance: ns = not significant; **=0.01; ***=0.001.

It may be a surprise, but there is no relationship between the two measures of risk tolerance and the outcomes. The average values on personal control of outcomes, responding to organizational challenges with an innovative or adaptive strategy, or the measure of economic sophistication, are virtually identical for the three outcomes. Why is there not a greater relationship to outcomes? Several issues are relevant. First, because of the limitations on interview space, many of the multi-item measures had few items and moderate reliability. Measurement error, or imprecision, could reduce the relationships. Second, all motivational and personal features were measured at the beginning of the process. Outcomes were identified over the following six years. Two things may have occurred during this period. Other, more influential factors such as start-up activities, could have affected the outcomes. It is also possible that motivations and personal orientations could have changed. Examples of such adjustments are discussed next.

Stability of Motivations

It is quite possible that the nascent entrepreneurs adjusted or modified their preferences or judgments during the start-up process. Two examples illustrate the extent of these shifts.

Contextual motivation: shifts over time
Respondents were asked about their judgments regarding the context and their motivation over five follow-up interviews. These responses about the effect of context are not stable, as illustrated in Figure 4.3, which shows the changes in responses at annual intervals over six years following the initial interview.

The top five bars show the responses of those indicating the attraction of a business opportunity in the first interview. About 5% report that given the situation at the time of the fifth follow-up interview, they now consider business creation their best choice for work. Over 90% continue to emphasize the importance of the business opportunity.

The bottom five bars of Figure 4.3 show the responses of those that indicated business creation as their best choice in the first interview. In the follow-up interviews from 30% to 50% have changed and, at the time of the fifth follow-up interview, consider the business opportunity the main attraction.

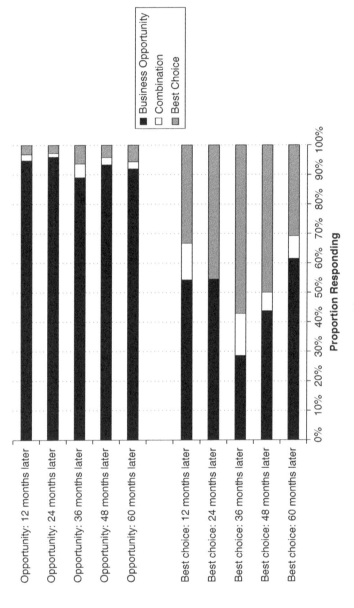

Figure 4.3   Contextual motivation: stability over time[42]

Both shifts may reflect adjustments in the expectations for the nascent venture; it may look more or less promising. There may also be changes in other work options, or the job market may be more or less favorable.

Entrepreneurial intensity: shifts over time

Business creation can be a lengthy process; maintaining a high level of commitment over several years may be a challenge. Figure 4.4 shows the level of intensity in 13, 29, and 53 months after the initial interview. The three groups of bars represent the changes for those that had high, medium, and low levels of intensity in the first interview. There is a systematic reduction in entrepreneurial intensity. About one-third of those reflecting a high level of intensity in the initial interview have a reduced level 13 months later, and there is a further reduction to about half 53 months after the first interview. Regardless of whether the level of intensity was low, medium, or high in the initial interview, there is an increase in the proportion reflecting a low level of intensity in later interviews. A small proportion appear to get more committed during the start-up process.

While those involved in business creation reflect a stronger motivation to pursue entrepreneurship than typical adults, it is clear that a high level of commitment may be difficult to maintain.

These examples indicate that shifts in motivation and personal interests are very common, perhaps in reaction to other factors that are affecting the start-up process and the outcomes. Motivations and personal goals identified at the beginning may change significantly as the start-up process unfolds.

OVERVIEW

The most important conclusions from assessment of motivations and personal orientations of those involved in business creation are:

- If an "entrepreneurial personality" can be identified, it will not have a major effect on participation in business creation.
- In advanced countries, like the U.S., most nascent entrepreneurs are attracted (pulled) into the effort because of promising business opportunities; in developing countries up to half

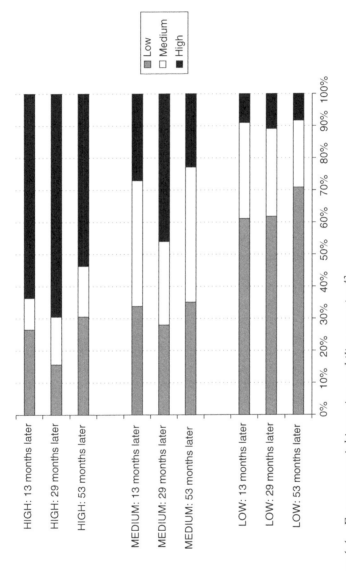

Figure 4.4   Entrepreneurial intensity: stability over time[43]

may be involved because they have no better choices for work (pushed).

- Contextual influences can vary over time, as nascent entrepreneurs adjust their judgments each year in response to changes in the attractiveness of the start-up venture and other options.
- Business creators are attracted to firm start-ups for personal work autonomy, wealth, a sense of achievement, and respect from their social contacts. The relative emphasis is not affected by gender, age, or prior workforce status.
- Nascent entrepreneurs reflect a higher need for achievement and commitment intensity than typical adults.
- Those involved in business creation are just as risk averse as typical adults. Those nascent entrepreneurs pursuing high growth ventures are more risk tolerant, but are unlikely to be candidates for Gamblers Anonymous.
- Growth oriented nascent entrepreneurs give slightly more emphasis to achieving work autonomy, wealth, task focus, desire for respect, greater tolerance for risk, and greater intensity, which are more consistent with the popular image of "real entrepreneurship."
- A stronger need for achievement, a less intense focus, intrinsic motivations, a preference for a growth business, and responding to business opportunities may be associated with developing a profitable venture.
- There is little evidence that a tolerance for risk, confidence in personal control of outcomes, decision-making strategies, or economic sophistication is related to creating profitable ventures.
- There is evidence that motivations and orientations may shift during the start-up process.

Overall, those engaged in business creation appear to be typical adults, each with a mixture of personal motives, responding to their situation at a unique point in their life course. Those interested in growth businesses are willing to accept some risk to achieve their ends, but this may be seen as a necessary cost rather than an effort to satisfy an urge to gamble.

Those interested in business creation need not worry about having an appropriate "personality."

POLICY IMPLICATIONS

Three features of the assessment minimize any implications for policy: the lack of major differences between typical adults and those involved in business creation; the absence of a major association between motivation or orientations and outcomes; and the evidence that motives and objectives may shift during the start-up process. This would suggest that assessments of the potential of a proposed venture should emphasize the specifics of the planned implementation, not the initial motivations and aspirations.

One feature is of some significance regarding the image of entrepreneurs. While many are oriented toward rewards, they are clearly "risk averse." Most involved in business creation are not reckless adventurers.

NOTES

1. PSED RESPID 328100272, fictitious name, edited for clarity.
2. PSED RESPID 328100279, fictitious names, edited for clarity.
3. PSED RESPID 328100359, fictitious names, edited for clarity.
4. PSED RESPID 337800026, fictitious name, edited for clarity.
5. Based coding of open ended Wave A responses to item A2 (variables AA2A and AA2b) of the representative sample of those active in firm creation identified in PSED II. Weights based on those with outcome data and adjusted to account for bias in sampling and duration in the start-up process. First response represents 852 cases; second response represents 540 cases.
6. Evans and Leighton (1989) inference about participants in business creation.
7. PSED RESPID 328100124.
8. PSED RESPID 328100193.
9. PSED RESPID 328100156.
10. PSED RESPID 328100203.
11. PSED RESPID 328100204.
12. Based on PSED II wave A items AT1 and AT6 and cases with follow-up outcomes, weights adjusted to compensate for biases in sampling and duration in the start-up process (n=810).
13. A revision of patterns with new weights initially presented in Reynolds and Curtin (2008), Table 5.7.
14. Based on analysis reported in Reynolds (2011b, 2012a, 2015).
15. Discussed at some length in Reynolds (2012b).
16. Based on PSED I items QG1B AND QG1F and PSED II items AAW2 and AAW5; Cronbach's Alpha is 0.64.
17. Based on PSED I items QG1G, QG1K, and QG1N and PSED II items AAW6, AAW9, and AAW12; Cronbach's Alpha is 0.79.
18. Based on PSED I items QG1A, QG1L, QG1M, QG1O, and QG1Q and PSED II items AAW1, AAW10, AAW11, AAW13, and AAW14; Cronbach's Alpha is 0.76.

19. Based on PSED I items QG1D, QG1E, QG1I, and QG1J and PSED II items AAW3, AAW4, AAW7, and AAW8; Cronbach's Alpha is 0.69.
20. In the U.S. PSED I and II samples, an average of 29% claim the desire to be an entrepreneur came before the business idea, about 37% report that the business idea occurred first, and 35% claim that the idea and desire for business creation occurred simultaneously (Item QA2 in the PSED I data set and AA7 in the PSED II data set).
21. McClelland (1961).
22. Shaver (2004b) discusses the development of this index.
23. Items were from the PSED I mail questionnaire, QH3, QH5, QH6, QH7, QL1A, and QL1C. As they involved a five-point scale, QL1A and QL1C were dichotomized. Removing QH4, QH8, and QL1B, mentioned in the Shaver (2004b) commentary, improved the Cronbach Alpha reliability to 0.33.
24. Weighted to represent typical adults. Nascent entrepreneur weights adjusted for bias in sampling and duration in the start-up process (n=754). Same weights used to compare easy to manage and growth oriented nascent entrepreneurs (n=412).
25. This is item QH9 in the PSED I data set; the choices are labeled ALPHA (Sleepwell) and BETA (Eatwell).
26. There are two versions in the PSED I data set: QH1 refers to choices affected by personal skills and energy, and QH2 refers to choices affected by external events. The patterns are almost identical on the two items; the results for QH1 are presented in this text. Expected value is the payoff multiplied by the probability, which is $1 million for each option.
27. Typical adults weighted to represent the population. Nascent entrepreneur weights adjusted for bias in sampling and duration in the start-up process. Typical adults versus nascents involves 755 and 752 cases. Easy to manage versus growth nascents comparisons involves 413 and 409 cases. In the population, n=795 for top comparison, n=789 for the bottom.
28. Xu and Ruef (2004) provide a more comprehensive assessment of this issue.
29. This topic is discussed in detail in Liao and Welsch (2004).
30. Items were from PSED I mail questionnaire, QL1D, QL1E, QL1F, and QL1G, and the same items in the three subsequent follow-ups. The Cronbach's Alpha for standardized items was 0.58 for 452 cases of Wave 1 data, 0.69 for 317 cases of Wave 2 data, 0.63 for 268 cases of Wave 3 data, and 0.72 for 315 cases of Wave 4 data.
31. Typical adults weighted to represent the population. Nascent entrepreneur weights adjusted for bias in sampling and duration in the start-up process. Typical adults versus nascent comparison involves 758 cases. Easy to manage versus growth oriented entrepreneurs involves 415 cases.
32. Discussed in Shaver (2004a).
33. Items from PSED I mail questionnaire were QL1H, QL1I, and Ql1J. Cronbach's Alpha reliability was 0.49.
34. Johnson, Danis, and Dollinger (2004).
35. Weighted to represent typical adults. Nascent entrepreneur weights adjusted for sampling and duration in process bias. N varies from 752 to 758. Nascent entrepreneur comparisons involve from 411 to 415 cases.
36. Items were from PSED I phone interview schedule, Q327, Q328, and Q329. Item Q328 was recoded to three values by combining sometimes a poor match with often a poor match so all three items were trifurcated. Cronbach's Alpha reliability was 0.23.
37. Discussed in Morgan (2004).
38. Items from PSED I mail questionnaire were QL1K and QL1L. Cronbach's Alpha reliability was 0.13.

39. A recent review finds that 13 personality traits appear to explain from 1% to 10% of the variation in participation in business creation and business performance (Frese and Gielnik, 2014).
40. See Gartner (1989) for a review of the research on the "entrepreneurial personality" and the lack of systematic predictive success.
41. All cases weighted to adjust for bias in screening selection and duration in the start-up process. Growth orientation (n=1,415) and Intrinsic Motivation (n=1,249) include cases from both PSED I and II. Contextual motivation (n=813) includes cases from PSED II. Need for Achievement (n=395), Entrepreneurial Intensity (n=398), Risk Preference (n=398), Preferred Profit vs Risk (n=394), Personal Control of Outcomes (n=398), Innovative/Adaptive Decisions (n=564), and Economic Sophistication (n=395) based on PSED I cases.
42. PSED II cases (see note 12 above), weighted to adjust for bias in sampling and duration in the start-up process.
43. PSED I cases (see note 32 above), weighted to adjust for bias in sampling and duration in the start-up process.

5. It is a social experience

Business creation is inherently a social activity. The persistent myth of the solo economic gunslinger—taking on all comers in a competitive shootout—is just that, a myth. Few activities require more human contacts with customers, partners and employees, suppliers, supportive family and mentors, financiers, regulators and, to some extent, competitors. The start-up team and these social networks may be involved in close social relationships.

START-UP TEAMS

There are two ways to consider the start-up teams working with nascent ventures. The size and structure of start-up teams experienced by 16 million nascent entrepreneurs is presented in Figure 5.1, reflecting adjustments to compensate for different amounts of time in the start-up process.

About half are ventures where one person will own the new business and have sole responsibility for all activity. The other half will be in teams involving two to five other owners (excluding passive owners that may share ownership).[1]

Those with multiple owners include teams of spouses or other relatives and teams of colleagues collaborating to create the new business. Among the team efforts, 22% of nascent entrepreneurs are involved with their spouse. If family members or relatives on a team expect to own half or more of a new venture, it is considered a family team. They are 8% of all nascent ventures. Twenty-two percent will be involved with one (13%), two (5%), three (3%) or five or more (1%) colleagues. The percentage of nascent entrepreneurs involved with a "family start-up" is either 29%, the spousal pairs and family teams, or 77%, if the sole proprietors are assumed to have family support and are, therefore, considered family businesses. One-fifth (22%) of nascent entrepreneurs are

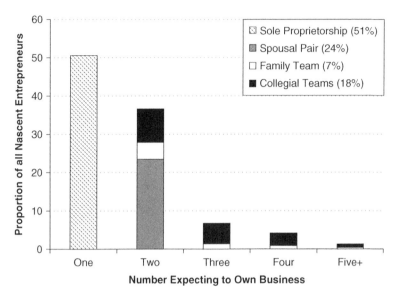

Figure 5.1   Nascent entrepreneurs: team size and social relationships[2]

involved in collegial teams; this is 43% of those involved with a start-up team.

The size and structure of ten million nascent ventures is somewhat different, as presented in Figure 5.2. These estimates require a different calculation, one that adjusts for the size of the start-up team and the time the venture is involved in the start-up process.

The major difference is the larger proportion of ventures that are one-person initiatives. While 48% of nascent entrepreneurs will experience business creation on their own, these account for 67% of the nascent ventures. Teams of spouses account for 15% and other family teams another 5% of nascent ventures. About 13% of nascent ventures are being implemented by collegial teams; collegial teams are 38% of all team led nascent ventures. Family start-ups are either 20% of all nascent ventures or, if sole proprietorship are included, 87% of all these ventures.

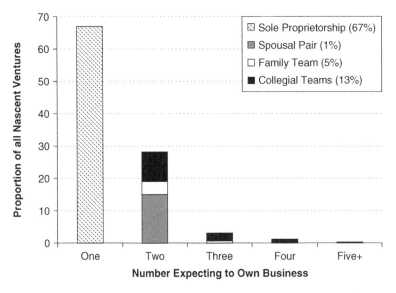

Figure 5.2   Nascent ventures: team size and social relationships[3]

START-UP TEAM ORGANIZATION

The types of activities emphasized by the start-up teams is reflected in assignments of specific responsibilities. Larger start-up teams can benefit from shared responsibilities for the administrative functions. The relative importance of a function is reflected in its assignment as a primary job responsibility. This is shown in Table 5.1, which presents assignment of primary responsibilities for different sized start-up teams.

The one-person start-up effort is the simplest; a single person is responsible for everything, and is identified as general management.

When two people expect to own the business, usually spouses or life partners, general management is a high priority with a specific assignment for half (52%) of the ventures, a responsibility of the first person in 55% and the second person in 49% of the cases. In some teams, both partners are general managers. Sales and marketing has the second highest priority, assigned in 21% of the cases. Other functions may get specific assignments, depending on the business idea and market in which the new firm will compete.

Table 5.1   Team member responsibilities by start-up team size[4]

	Person 1 (%)	Person 2 (%)	Person 3 (%)	Person 4 (%)	Average (%)
One Person Team					
General Management	100				100
Sales/Marketing/Service					
Finance/Accounting					
Technical/Research					
Operations/ Manufacturing					
Administration					
	100				
Two Person Team					
General Management	55	49			52
Sales/Marketing/Service	24	19			21
Finance/Accounting	3	12			8
Technical/Research	4	5			4
Operations/ Manufacturing	10	8			9
Administration	4	7			6
	100	100			100
Three Person Team					
General Management	55	18	33		35
Sales/Marketing/Service	21	38	23		27
Finance/Accounting	10	10	18		13
Technical/Research	3	11	7		7
Operations/ Manufacturing	4	14	14		11
Administration	7	9	5		7
	100	100	100		100
Four Person Team					
General Management	46	47	12	31	34
Sales/Marketing/Service	6	13	52	43	28
Finance/Accounting	26	4	10	6	12
Technical/Research	5	9	9	3	7
Operations/ Manufacturing	8	15	8	10	10
Administration	9	11	9	7	9
	100	99	100	100	100

Three and four-person teams have less emphasis on general management and greater emphasis on specific functions; a larger proportion have individuals responsible for marketing and sales. Finance and accounting and technical and research functions are more likely to be assigned to specific individuals in the larger teams. Larger start-up teams may reflect a more complex business operation, as there is more diversity in assignment of functions. Specific attention to individual functions may be one reason larger teams are more likely to reach profitability.

HELPFUL OTHERS

Many start-ups get help from a variety of people that will not share in the ownership of the new business. These examples reflect the diversity of assistance from helpful others:

> Walter was in the computer hardware business and helped us by providing discounted access to obsolete equipment.[5]

> Catherine has an MA in early childhood education and helped us meet the state requirement for the credentials required to open a daycare center.[6]

> Robert guaranteed our credit to a critical supplier so we got a discount from regular market pricing.[7]

> Martha provides moral support, suggests improvements, recommends volunteers, and she is in touch with developments at school with applications to our business.[8]

> Peter is part of the team and his dad let us set up on one of his properties in exchange for a share of the ownership.[9]

In addition to those that may provide assistance when needed or on an occasional basis, others become a full-time member of the start-up team without expecting to share in the ownership.[10]

A focus on the start-up teams gives the impression that half of start-ups are solo efforts. However, when helpful others are taken into consideration, presented in Table 5.2, only about one-fourth (27%) of nascent ventures involve one person going it alone; three-fourths involve contributions from one to six other persons. The truly lone entrepreneur is a rarity.

The proportion of start-up teams that have no outside help is

Table 5.2   Number of helpful mentors by start-up team structure

Start-up Structure	None (%)	One (%)	Two (%)	Three (%)	Four (%)	Five+ (%)	Total (%)	Average
Sole proprietor	27	35	12	15	5	7	101	1.5
Spousal pair	48	21	17	8	5	1	100	1.3
Family team	40	15	32	13	0	0	100	1.1
Collegial team	56	16	12	6	4	6	100	1.5
All	35	29	13	13	4	6	100	1.5

Table 5.3   Relationship to helping mentor[11]

	Sole Proprietor (%)	Spousal Pair (%)	Family Team (%)	Collegial Team (%)	All (%)
Friend, acquaintance	33	21	10	44	32
Family member, relative	19	47	73	17	24
Business associate	24	27	2	20	23
Spouse, partner	14	2	13	7	12
Other	10	3	2	11	9
	100	100	100	99	100

somewhat higher, but team efforts are social activities to begin with. Ironically, the average number of persons involved (1.5) is greatest for sole proprietors or collegial team.

The source of help, shown in Table 5.3, is most likely to be a personal friend (32% of the time) or a family member or relative (24%). Business associates (23%) are the next most common. Spouses or partners are frequently mentioned (12%) and teachers, counselors, or other individuals in the social network (9%) may also provide assistance, advice or support. Family members and relatives are more likely to assist spousal pairs or family teams. Friends or business associates are frequently involved with collegial teams or sole proprietorships.

These supportive mentors, friends, and associates provide a wide range of assistance, presented in Table 5.4. The most common

Table 5.4   Assistance provided by helping mentor[12]

	Sole Proprietor (%)	Spousal Pair (%)	Family Team (%)	Collegial Team (%)	All (%)
Advice, ideas, information	41	44	65	25	41
Access to finance	13	4	8	19	12
Introductions	11	14	8	12	11
Business services	9	11	5	31	11
Access to physical assets	11	8	0	4	10
Informal business training	8	13	0	1	8
Personal services	4	6	11	7	5
Other, multiple	2	0	3	1	2
	99	100	100	100	100

form of help is advice, ideas, and information for the nascent venture, mentioned in two of five cases (41%). Other forms of assistance commonly mentioned includes facilitating access to external financial support (12%), introductions to others that may facilitate the start-up (11%), providing business services such as accounting or legal assistance (11%), or helping gain access to physical resources such as office space or equipment (10%), and informal training in business skills (8%). There are, in addition, those that provide personal services, such as childcare or help with daily challenges (7%).

The mixture of assistance is similar for the sole proprietors, spousal pairs and family teams. For the non-family teams, emphasis is on access to finance, introductions, and business services, with less emphasis on advice, ideas, and information.

Note that while access to external finance is frequently mentioned as a primary challenge for start-ups, it is not the dominant form of help. This reflects the high proportion of start-up efforts that receive most of their initial financial support from the start-up team (discussed in Chapter 10).

PERSONAL INVOLVEMENT AND OUTCOMES

Start-ups with more people involved are more likely to reach initial profitability. This impact is reflected in two ways. First, as shown in Figure 5.3, over half of collegial teams (54%) and two in five (40%) family teams reach initial profitability, compared to one-third (33%) sole proprietorships and spousal pairs (33%). The proportion that have quit or disengaged is similar for all four types of structure, albeit slightly lower for collegial teams. The reduction in the proportion still active reflects variation among those achieving initial profitability.

The second reflection of the impact of more assistance involves considering all those involved: team members, helpers, and mentors. The impact of a larger number of total supporters, start-up team, and helpful others on the outcome is presented in Figure 5.4.

Among nascent ventures with five or more in the support group almost three in five (58%) reach initial profitability; only one-fourth (28%) report quitting. Among solo efforts, where only one person is

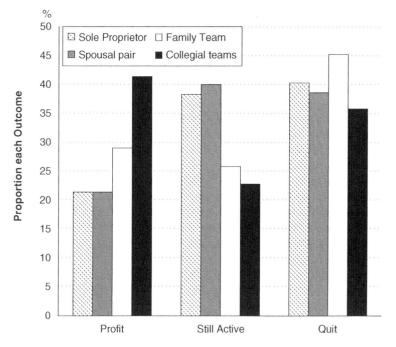

Figure 5.3   Team structure and outcomes[13]

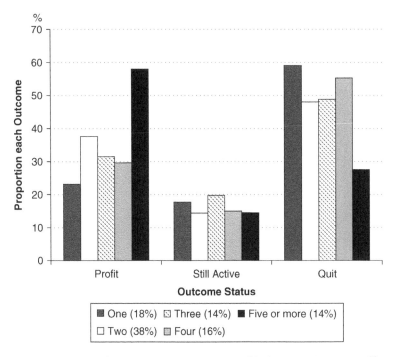

Figure 5.4   Total persons, start-up team and helpers, and outcomes[14]

involved, less than one-fourth (23%) reach initial profitability. Those ventures that involve from two to four individuals have intermediate success. Clearly, having more people increases the potential for achieving initial profitability.

But what types of assistance are the most helpful? Each start-up can be considered in terms of the assistance provided by the first helper mentioned in the interview. These are ranked in terms of the proportion of cases reaching profitability in Figure 5.5. Three types of assistance are associated with over one-third reaching profitability: access to physical assets (49%), provision of business services (43%), and advice, ideas, and information (36%). The two next most associated with reaching profitability are help with access to finance (31%) and introductions to others that can help the business (31%). Three other types of assistance are less associated with profitability, such as informal business training (26%) and provision of personal services (15%).

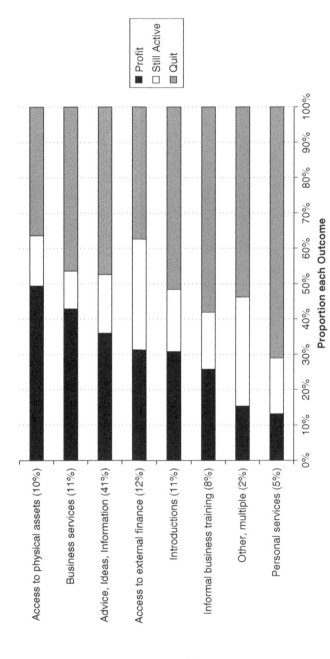

Figure 5.5 Type of helper assistance and outcomes[15]

OVERVIEW

Consideration of the social relationships, both within the start-up team and from outside helpers, indicates that:

- Half of nascent entrepreneurs expect to be the sole owner of the new business; seven in ten nascent ventures are anticipated to be one-person businesses.
- Thirty percent of nascent entrepreneurs are in teams of families or relatives; these are 20% of all nascent ventures.
- One-fifth of nascent entrepreneurs are in collegial teams; these are 13% of all nascent ventures.
- Very few start-ups are solo efforts without outside assistance; only one-fourth of all nascent entrepreneurs are on their own with no help from outsiders.
- In larger start-up teams more individuals are assigned to different functions, particularly sales and marketing.
- Collegial teams are most likely to reach initial profitability, followed by family based teams. Sole proprietorships and spousal pairs are least likely to reach profitability.
- Helpful persons, friends, family members, and business associates provide a variety of assistance to start-up teams. Advice, ideas, and information are the most frequent forms of assistance, followed by help in gaining access to finance, introductions to critical stakeholders, business training, and business services.
- The more individuals involved the greater the potential for reaching profitability. This would include both those on the start-up teams and outside mentors and helpers.
- Nascent ventures helped by those that facilitate access to physical assets, business services, and information and advice are most likely to reach profitability, although other forms of assistance can also be helpful.

Starting a new firm is very much a social effort; the more individuals that are involved the greater the likelihood of success.

POLICY IMPLICATIONS

Pursuing business creation is a social activity. Just as those seeking employment are more successful when they have a large social network,[16] nascent entrepreneurs that get others involved are more likely to reach profitability. It may also reduce the stress associated with an initiative fraught with uncertainty. Efforts to promote business creation may be more effective if they encourage nascent entrepreneurs to make wide use of their social networks.

NOTES

1. In the representative sample of nascent ventures identified in the PSED I and II projects. Cases with more than five potential owner–managers are rare; they are combined with the five-person teams. About 5% of the cases involve ownership by other businesses or financial institutions. These juristic entities are ignored for this assessment.
2. This is based on representative samples of start-up ventures identified in the U.S. in 1999 and 2005. Case weights are adjusted to compensate for sampling bias only (n=1,428).
3. This is based on representative samples of start-up ventures identified in the U.S. in 1999 and 2005. Case weights are adjusted to compensate for bias related to sampling, start-up team size, and duration in the start-up process (n=1,417).
4. Based on U.S. PSED II data file, responsibilities associated with first four team members in Wave A, items AH19_1 (n=292), AH19_2 (n=251), AH19_3 (n=31), and AH19_4 (n=10). Five-person teams excluded due to the small number of cases with complete data. Case weights adjusted to compensate for bias in sampling, team size, and duration in the start-up process.
5. RESPID 328100294, fictitious name.
6. RESPID 328100634, fictitious name.
7. RESPID 328100656, fictitious name.
8. RESPID 328200125, fictitious name.
9. RESPID 328100294, fictitious name.
10. These were tracked separately in the PSED II interviews. These key non-owners are combined with helpful others for this presentation.
11. First mentor mentioned by team member 1 in PSED II Wave A. Case weights adjusted to compensate for bias in sampling, team size, and duration in the start-up process.
12. First mentor mentioned by team member 1 in PSED II Wave A. Case weights adjusted to compensate for bias in sampling, team size, and duration in the start-up process.
13. Based on PSED I and II cases with data on outcomes. Weights adjusted to compensate for bias in sampling, start-up team size, and duration in the start-up process (n=1,417).
14. Based on PSED I and II cases with data on outcome. Weights adjusted to compensate for bias in sampling, start-up team size, and duration in the start-up process (n=1,418).

15. Assessment based on the major form of assistance provided by the first person mentioned as providing assistance to the start-up initiative. Based on PSED I and II cases with data on outcomes. Weights adjusted to compensate for bias in sampling, start-up team size, and duration in the start-up process (n=1,419).
16. Granovetter (1955).

6. Know what you are doing

Entrepreneurial ventures offering new things, such as ride-sharing or cheap online access to movies, get a lot of attention. But the vast majority of start-ups enter established markets with substantial competition. This provides a major dilemma for nascent entrepreneurs. Established firms are not eager to share customers. Knowing how to manage a firm as a successful competitor is one of the critical components for success. There are several ways to develop this expertise. One is to work in the industry in which the new firm will compete. Another is to take classes, seminars, or workshops to develop expertise in how to implement and manage a new firm. A third option is to get help and assistance from the large variety of agencies and services currently available for those creating new businesses. All these strategies for developing entrepreneurial skills have a positive effect.

NEW FIRMS AND THEIR ECONOMIC SECTOR

Virtually all, over 99%, of nascent ventures can be assigned to an existing economic sector. This is a strong indicator that they will have competitors, businesses that were the basis for defining these market sectors. The proportion of these start-ups in each sector are compared with existing businesses in Table 6.1. Counts of existing businesses come from two sources. One provides a count of sole proprietorships based on individual federal tax returns. The other a count of firms with employees based on federal social security payments. There are some variations in the proportions in each sector. For example, there are more firms with employees (8% of the total) in food services (restaurants) than sole proprietorships (1%); it is hard to be a one-person restaurant.

There are, however, nascent ventures in every sector and the overall distributions are very similar. This reflects, of course, the strong tendency of individuals to gain experience in an industry and, once

Table 6.1   Sector distribution: nascent ventures and established firms

NAICS[a]		Nascent Ventures[1] (%)	Sole Proprietorships[2] (%)	Firms with Employees[3] (%)
11	Agriculture, Forestry, Fishing, & Hunting	1.8	1.2	0.4
21	Mining	0.0	0.5	0.3
22	Utilities	1.8	0.1	0.1
23	Construction	7.7	12.2	12.6
31–33	Manufacturing	4.8	1.6	4.9
42	Wholesale Trade	3.1	2.0	5.7
44–45	Retail Trade	22.5	9.7	12.4
48–49	Transportation & Warehousing	2.5	4.7	2.8
51	Information	7.0	1.5	1.3
52	Finance & Insurance	6.4	3.7	4.2
53	Real Estate & Rental & Leasing	3.9	11.4	4.8
54	Professional, Scientific, & Technical Services	12.7	14.0	12.4
55	Management of Companies & Enterprises	0.0	0.0	0.4
56	Administration & Support; Waste Management & Remediation	3.0	6.8	5.2
61	Educational Services	2.6	2.1	1.2
62	Health Care & Social Assistance	4.8	8.2	9.9
71	Arts, Entertainment, and Recreation	2.2	4.7	1.9
72	Accommodation & Food Services	2.9	1.4	7.6
81	Consumer Services	9.6	14.3	11.3
92	Public Administration	0.2	0.0	0.0
99	Unclassified	0.6	0.0	0.7
		100.0	100.1	100.1

Note: a. See National Technical Information Service, 2002.

they see a promising opportunity, take steps to create a business in the same economic sector.

This also indicates that very few new businesses will have no competition for customers. All start-ups need to be prepared to compete for customers; the more traditional the business the more intense the competition.

PRIOR EXPERIENCE

Peter has been working in facilities management for 15 years and sees a need for this service among smaller companies.[4]

Harry had been in the securities industry for 20 years and needed to make money during retirement.[5]

Andrew started painting with his uncle 18 years ago and likes to make places look better.[6]

Charles worked in a tax accounting service for 12 years, was unhappy with his employer, and is going out on his own this year.[7]

Sara had ten years of experience working for somebody else and decided it was time to start the Feel Good Hair Salon.[8]

These are some of the many examples of individuals that first developed expertise and experience before entering business creation.[9] Work experience is a major source of business ideas, and business ideas that seem to have greater potential. About two-fifths (38%) of nascent ventures are based on business ideas or opportunities recognized from current or previous work experience. Another third (36%) reflect experience with managing another business or participation in another start-up effort. A hobby or personal interest is the source of one-fifth (22%) and one in 25 (4%) reflect research activities.

The source of the business idea is related to the outcome of the start-up process, and is summarized in Table 6.2.

Over one-third (35–40%) of the nascent ventures based on ideas developed from current or prior work experience, or other businesses or start-up efforts, reach initial profitability, compared to one-fourth (23%) that reflect an interest in a hobby or one-sixth (16%) that emerge from research and development experiences. This would suggest that knowing the business arena facilitates creating profitable firms.

But work experience can provide more than just a business idea;

Table 6.2   Source of business ideas and outcomes[10]

Source of Business Idea	Proportion (%)	Initial Profitability (%)	Still Active (%)	Quit (%)	Row Totals (%)
Current, prior work experience	38.5	39.9	16.6	43.6	100.1
Other business or start-up effort	35.7	35.4	8.9	55.6	99.9
Hobby	22.0	22.6	14.0	63.4	100.0
Research and development	3.8	15.6	9.4	75.0	100.0
All	100.0	33.6	13.0	53.4	100.0

Note: Statistically significant at 0.000.

Table 6.3   Team same industry work experience and outcomes[11]

Same Industry Work Experience	Proportion (%)	Initial Profitability (%)	Still Active (%)	Quit (%)	Row Totals (%)
None	25.0	31.9	9.9	58.2	100.0
1–5 years	23.0	25.8	15.6	58.6	100.0
6–10 years	15.2	23.6	25.9	50.5	100.0
11–30 years	28.9	45.1	17.1	37.8	100.0
31+ years	7.9	65.2	11.6	23.2	100.0
All	100.0	35.7	15.9	48.4	100.0

Note: Statistically significant at 0.000.

it also provides information about the competitive arena and the network of relationships with suppliers, those providing financial support, and the specific regulatory context. One of the advantages of a team effort is the potential for pooling the collective experience of the team. This can be a major benefit to the initiative.

While one-fourth of start-up teams have no same industry work experience, Table 6.3 indicates that over one-third (37%) share 11 or more years of same industry experience. More than a third (38%) have from one to ten years of experience. Ventures initiated by teams with more experience in the start-up sector are more likely to reach initial profitability, as shown in Table 6.3.

Work experience in the industry appears to have a step function impact on profitability. The proportion of nascent ventures led by start-up teams with less than six years of experience that reach profitability is slightly below average (26–32%). In contrast, 45 to 65% of those ventures launched by teams with 11 or more years of same industry experience reach initial profitability. The intermediate same industry experience group, teams with 6–10 years of start-up experience, have lower proportions in profit (24%), but one-quarter (26%) are still active in the start-up process.

Greater team same industry work experience is also associated with substantial reductions in the proportion that disengage, from 58% among those ventures with no same industry experience to 23% among those with over 30 years of same industry experience. These more experienced teams may be involved in more complicated initiatives that take longer to reach a clear outcome.

Same industry work experience has an impact on the outcomes. In contrast, general work experience appears to be unrelated to the outcomes.

Previous experience with business creation can provide different, complementary skills. It is useful to consider the total experience of all team members. As presented in Table 6.4, no member of about two-fifths (43%) of the teams have any start-up experience. For about

Table 6.4   Team start-up experience and outcomes[12]

Other Start-up Experiences	Proportion (%)	Initial Profitability (%)	Still Active (%)	Quit (%)	Row Totals (%)
None	43.1	33.7	11.8	54.6	100.1
One	16.9	34.2	12.5	53.3	100.0
Two, three	16.3	29.9	25.1	45.0	100.0
Four to nine	8.8	34.4	23.2	42.4	100.0
Ten+	14.8	50.5	17.1	32.4	100.0
All	99.9	35.7	15.9	48.4	100.0

Note: Statistically significant at 0.000.

Table 6.5   Team work and start-up experience and outcomes[13]

Same Industry Work and Start-up Experiences	Prevalence (%)	Initial Profitability (%)	Still Active (%)	Quit (%)	Row Totals (%)
0–5 years work, 0–1 start-ups	37.7	32.3	10.3	57.4	100.0
0–5 years work, 2+ start-ups	10.2	17.2	21.4	61.4	100.0
6+ years work, 0–1 start-ups	22.5	36.4	15.0	48.6	100.0
6+ years work, 2+ start-ups	29.6	46.0	21.9	32.1	100.0
All	100.0	35.7	15.9	48.3	99.9

Note: Statistically significant at 0.000.

one-third (33%), teams share from one to three previous efforts and for one-fourth (24%), teams share four or more previous ventures.

The major impact of a team with more start-up experience is a reduction in the proportion that have abandoned the effort (Table 6.4). The proportion of quits decreases from 55% for teams with no other start-up experience to 32% among teams with ten or more start-ups in the background. Half (50%) of teams with ten or more previous start-up experiences reach profitability, compared to one-third of teams with less experience. Ventures initiated by teams with two to nine prior experiences, however, are more likely to still be involved in the start-up process. Again, business experiences may lead to more complex and significant efforts, which take longer to implement.

The joint impact of these two types of background experience is presented in Table 6.5. In this table, both types of team background are bifurcated. About two-fifths (38%) have little same industry work or start-up experiences. About three-tenths (30%) have considerable same industry and previous start-up experience. The remainder are intermediate, with varying mixtures on both types of experience.

Ventures led by teams with the most experience are more likely to reach profitability (46%) or be active in the start-up process (22%) and less likely to have disengaged (32%). Over half of those in two low experience categories have abandoned the nascent venture. This confirms that the joint impact of these two types of experiences leads to a better outcome.

CLASSROOM EXPERIENCE

Another source of expertise is taking courses related to business management. These may include sales and marketing, accounting and financial control, production or plant management, human resource management, inventory control and distribution, financial and capital management, and management of technology or innovation. Based on information related to the respondent, team member one, Table 6.6 indicates that two-thirds of these nascent entrepreneurs have taken one or more relevant courses and one-quarter have taken ten or more business courses.

While the patterns in Table 6.6 are not statistically significant, the results suggest that exposure to business courses is associated with reaching profitability. Nascent ventures where team member one has taken four or more courses are more likely to reach profitability than those where there is less classroom experience. Ventures where the principal has not taken any business courses are the most likely to quit. It may be that classroom exposure would be more effective if combined with internships or supervised experiences in real life businesses, which has a positive impact on reaching profitability.

A similar improvement is found among those that have completed

Table 6.6   Number of business administration courses and outcomes[14]

Classroom Experience	Prevalence (%)	Initial Profitability (%)	Still Active (%)	Quit (%)	Row Totals (%)
None	33.9	33.9	18.5	47.6	100.0
1 to 3 courses	24.0	36.4	22.7	40.9	100.0
4 to 9 courses	16.7	44.3	19.7	36.1	100.1
10 or more courses	25.4	40.9	16.1	43.0	100.0
All	100.0	38.0	19.1	42.9	100.0

Note: Not statistically significant at 0.05 level.

courses in mathematics or economics, suggesting that comfort with quantitative subject matter may also facilitate business creation.

HELPING AGENCIES

There is a variety of consulting and advisory services established to facilitate U.S. business creation and small business management. The best known may be the widespread network of Small Business Development Centers (SBDC), although most states have hundreds of programs available for nascent entrepreneurs. An effort to create a comprehensive list in Wisconsin in 1993 identified 456 different programs providing 752 unique forms of assistance.[15] Most don't charge for the assistance. These consulting services are a source of formal assistance from unbiased experts whose major concern is the establishment of successful businesses.

It is rare for those implementing new ventures to have contact with any helping agencies. As summarized in Table 6.7, over four-fifths (84%) do not report any helping agency contact as they begin the start-up process. A little more than one-tenth (12%) report up to nine hours of assistance, one in 33 (3%) from 10 to 39 hours of help, and one in 70 (1.4%), 40 or more hours.

It turns out that assistance from these sources is associated with a larger proportion of nascent ventures that achieve initial profitability—or at least do not disengage from the effort. Table 6.7 presents the relationship between the number of hours spent with the last helping agency contacted and the outcomes for the venture.

Table 6.7   Consulting agencies assistance and outcomes[16]

Agency Assistance	Prevalence (%)	Initial Profitability (%)	Still Active (%)	Quit (%)	Row Totals (%)
None	83.7	34.9	20.9	44.2	100.0
1–9 hours	11.9	71.6	10.4	17.9	99.9
10–39 hours	3.0	52.9	11.8	35.3	100.0
40+ hours	1.4	12.5	50.0	37.5	100.0
All	100.0	39.5	19.8	40.7	100.0

Note: Statistically significant at 0.000.

While 35% of those that did not make contact are associated with a nascent venture that reached initial profitability, the proportion of those that spend from one to nine hours with the consultants that achieved initial profitability is doubled (72%) and is 50% higher (53%) among those that spend 10 to 39 hours. The small number (12) that reported spending over 40 hours are distinctive. While only 12% report initial profitability, half (50%) are still in the start-up process. This suggests that either they have complex businesses to implement or they were poorly prepared to enter the start-up process and needed a lot of coaching.

The relationship between involvement with helping agencies and reaching a profitable outcome is compelling. This may reflect useful assistance provided to nascent ventures or it may be that start-up teams with the potential to launch a profitable firm may also have been savvy about using available expertise. There is no evidence that contact with helping agencies is a disadvantage.

OVERVIEW

> With an MA in public administration and 33 years of management experience Solomon Management Consulting should do well.[17]

> With 20 years' experience cooking barbeque with my own recipe, Sammy's Ribs should be a success.[18]

> We have a very experienced team and have done a lot of research. If we all work together we can't help but be successful in construction.[19]

Expertise has a major impact on confidence in business creation and the outcome of implementing a new firm. This overview suggests that:

- Most new businesses enter established markets with established competitors.
- Nascent ventures based on business ideas reflecting work experience are more likely to reach initial profitability.
- Nascent venture teams with more same industry experience are more likely to reach initial profitability.
- Nascent venture teams with more start-up experience are more likely to reach initial profitability.
- Nascent ventures guided by individuals with more business

administration coursework may be more likely to reach initial profitability.

- Nascent ventures receiving assistance from helping agencies may be more likely to reach initial profitability.

In sum, there is nothing more important than knowing the industry, business practices, and competitive environment in which the new firm will operate. This is far more significant than the personal background, motives, or personal orientation of the start-up team.

The small minority of entrepreneurial ventures that create new goods or services, where there is no well-defined market or competition, are in a different situation. There is no industry experience to acquire. In this unique situation, the start-up team has the advantage of being first and has as much expertise as anybody. The major challenge is to convince potential customers that the firm provides something of value; success will lead to the definition of a new economic sector. Effective teams will be the first to define a role in the new market and maintain a first mover advantage. On the other hand, the procedures and skills to manage a business, even with a unique, unprecedented product, can be helpful in creating a more efficient operation. A background in business management can be an asset.

POLICY IMPLICATIONS

Knowing what you are doing has a strong association with achieving profitability. Candidate nascent entrepreneurs should be encouraged to acquire the skills and experience associated with managing a business, new or otherwise. This is particularly important for those entering existing markets. This can be provided in standard educational settings, specialized workshops or seminars, work experience in established firms, or with specialized coaching or mentoring services. A combination of programs, such as classroom training combined with supervised internships in real businesses, may improve outcomes. All sources of increased expertise increases the proportion of nascent ventures that will become profitable. There is no substitute for knowing what you are doing.

NOTES

1. PSED ventures, 1999 and 2005 cohorts, weight adjusted to compensate for bias in sampling, start-up team size, and start-up process duration (n=1,418).
2. U.S. Small Business Administration (2007), p. 307, for 2004 (n=19,523,741).
3. U.S. Small Business Administration (2007), p. 307, for 2004 (n=5,657,774).
4. PSED I RESPID 328100003, fictitious name.
5. PSED I RESPID 328100011, fictitious name.
6. PSED I RESPID 328100104, fictitious name.
7. PSED I RESPID 328100459, fictitious name.
8. PSED I RESPID 337800161, fictitious names.
9. Based on PSED II cohort, item AA9.
10. Based on PSED II cohort, recoding of item AA9. All cases with known outcome. Weights adjusted to compensate for bias in sampling, start-up team size, and start-up process duration (n=846).
11. PSED I and II same industry work experience aggregated across teams. All cases with known outcome. Weights adjusted to compensate for bias in sampling, start-up team size, and start-up process duration.
12. PSED I and II start-up experiences aggregated across teams. All cases with known outcome. Weights adjusted to compensate for bias in sampling, start-up team size, and start-up process duration (n=1,418).
13. PSED I and II start-up experiences and same industry work experiences aggregated across teams. All cases with known outcome. Weights adjusted to compensate for bias in sampling, start-up team size, and start-up process duration (n=1,419).
14. PSED I mail questionnaire items, total of reports for team member 1 to items QF1A1, QF1B1, QF1C1, QF1D1, QF1E1, QFQF1, and QF1G1. All cases with known outcome. Weights adjusted to compensate for bias in sampling, start-up team size, and start-up process duration (n=366).
15. Reynolds, White, and others (1993).
16. Based on PSED I item Q309, number of hours of contact with most recent helping agency consulted. All cases with known outcome. Weights adjusted to compensate for bias in sampling, start-up team size, and start-up process duration (n=565).
17. PSED I RESPID 328100290, fictitious name.
18. PSED I RESPID 328100577, fictitious name.
19. PSED I RESPID 337800114.

7.   Do it!

How do nascent entrepreneurs create a business? They do things! Popular start-up activities are summarized in Table 7.1. They are ordered by the proportion of nascent ventures where they have been initiated. The rightmost column indicates those that occurred in the first month of the start-up process. While many more start-up activities could be added, these are many of the most common and important.[1]

Some activities are clearly more popular than others. Everybody gives serious thought to their nascent venture; it is reported by all those active in business creation. But serious thought is not action, and many talk the talk but don't even take the first steps to walk the walk. Hence, it is more useful to focus on what is done to create a new firm. These activities, however, vary in character. Some are a one-time event, such as establishing a business phone number or registration with a government agency, while others are a continuous activity, such as developing financial projections or promotion of the products, which may be adjusted as additional information becomes available. For this reason, the focus is on tracking initiation of a start-up activity, not when it is completed.

The most common activities include entrepreneurs investing money in the venture, developing procedures for delivering the product or service, defining the customer base, acquiring supplies, material, or inventory, and developing a business plan. Others, such as seeking external funding or applying for legal recognition of intellectual property, like a patent, trademark, or copyright, are less likely to be initiated. They may not be relevant for many nascent ventures.

There is, in addition, no one way to proceed. The rightmost column of Table 7.1 makes it clear that some teams started their effort with at least one of the activities. Most remarkable, a few report serious thought was initiated after they began the start-up process. Virtually every start-up activity is chosen as the first step in creating a new business by a start-up team. The most efficient

Table 7.1   Start-up activities by popularity[2]

Start-up Activity	Proportion Reporting (%)	Proportion in First Month (%)
Give serious thought to the nascent venture	100	90[a]
Principal invests own money	88	36
Develop model, procedure for delivery of output	82	27
Define markets or customer base	81	26
Acquire supplies, materials, inventory	78	20
Begin to develop a business plan	74	30
Begin marketing, promotion	73	17
Receive initial income from sales	72	12
Acquire, lease capital assets (land, building, equipment)	68	10
Develop financial projections	58	10
Establish phone line, internet listing	56	11
Obtain supplier credit	49	9
Register new firm with government	47	12
Principal begins devoting full-time to the start-up	42	9
Ask for external funding	32	5
Organize start-up team	31	7
Hire an employee	27	2
Receive external financial support	18	1
Seek intellectual property rights (patent, trademark, copyright)	18	1

Note: a. For initial thought, the proportion of any time up to and including the first month.

strategy for implementation may vary from one nascent venture to another, depending upon the nature of the business, the competitive context, and the available resources.

TIMING OF START-UP ACTIVITIES

When do nascent entrepreneurs initiate these activities? A summary of the timing for implementation for typical nascent ventures is presented in Figure 7.1. The dark bars associated with each activity

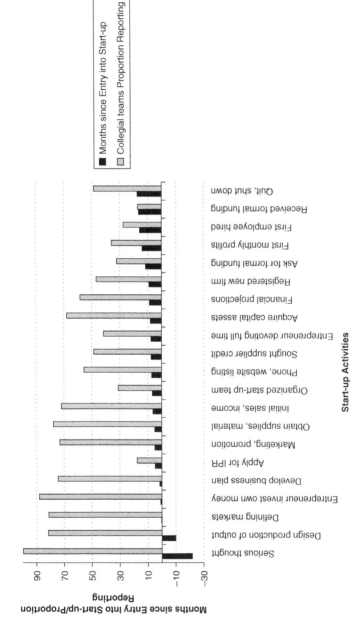

Note: IPR = intellectual property rights.

Figure 7.1 Prevalence and timing of start-up activities[3]

represents the number of months after entry into the process when the activity is initiated. The light bars represent the proportion that report initiating the activity.

Serious thought, which is not used to identify entry into the start-up process, occurs on average about 22 months before entering the start-up process with an activity. Several activities are very common at the beginning of the process: creating a model or procedure for delivery of the output, defining the market or customer base to be served, and investments of funds by the nascent entrepreneurs. Within the first six months, most have begun to develop a business plan, begun to market or promote their output, and started to assemble supplies, material or inventory. The small proportion (18%) that seek intellectual property rights (IPR) do so within five months. Between six months and a year, nascent entrepreneurs begin to receive their first income from sales, begin to organize a start-up team, establish a phone and website listing, seek supplier credit, begin to devote full-time to the venture, begin to acquire capital assets, and start to produce financial projections. For the 47% that register the new venture, which can be a first filing of state unemployment taxes, federal social security or income tax payments, or applying for a Federal EIN, this occurs about nine months after beginning the process. The 32% that seek formal funding tend to start this effort at the end of the first year.

Monthly profitability, to the far right of Figure 7.1, is reported by about one-third (36%) slightly more than a year (14 months) after beginning the process. But this is an average figure, and there is considerable variation among those that achieve profitability.

Activities that typically occur at the beginning of the second year include the first employee hiring and receipt of formal financing.

The half (48%) that disengage from the nascent venture, tend to do so at about 17 months after beginning the process.

This summary, to be sure, represents patterns typical of a representative sample of nascent ventures. There is dramatic variation among individual ventures associated with industry sector, the complexity of the venture, the geographic location, and the background of the start-up team. Nonetheless, this makes it clear that it takes a while to implement the activities required for business creation. While some new firms launch very quickly, many take several years to get all the components in place.

START-UP ACTIVITY AND OUTCOMES

Nascent entrepreneurs would prefer to reach profitability and to do so as quickly as possible. Most are realistic about the risk associated with their initiative and would like to know—sooner rather than later—if it isn't going to work out. It turns out that when the start-up activities for firms with different outcomes are compared, clear patterns emerge, as shown in Figure 7.2.

The most obvious pattern is that profitable ventures implement more activities—an average of 11 in the first 36 months. There is not much difference in the first month, but as early as three months those that continue in the start-up mode have less activity than the ventures with clear outcomes, either profitability or discontinuation. After six months, the profitable ventures are reporting more start-up activities than those that, later on, quit or continue in the process. After a year, there is little difference between those that eventually quit or continue to be active in the start-up process.

Nascent ventures that reach initial profitability implement more

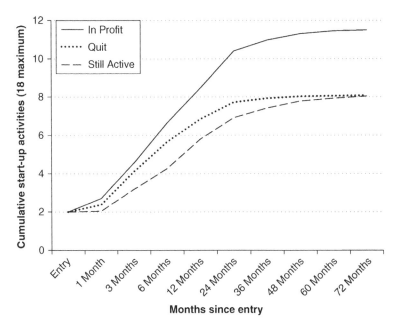

Figure 7.2   Total start-up activity and outcomes[4]

start-up activities. This may reflect, however, positive feedback and encouragement to these start-up teams as they proceed with the start-up process. As information that the venture may be successful is received, the start-up team may pursue a greater variety of start-up activities. Other teams that do not get positive encouragement may become discouraged, or realistic about the potential for the venture, and decline to implement more activities.

START-UP ACTIVITY AND TIME TO OUTCOMES

It is very useful to know the outcome for a nascent venture as quickly as possible. A shorter time in the start-up process reduces the sunk cost associated with the nascent venture. This will increase the return on investment in time and money for those ventures that reach profitability and minimize the losses for those that are abandoned. Considering only those nascent ventures that become profitable, the relationship between implementing start-up activities during the first three years and the average time required to reach profitability is presented in Figure 7.3. The vertical axis represents the time from entry to initial profitability; the horizontal axis the months since entry into the process that start-up activities are initiated. The five lines represent the amount of start-up activity initiated.

In this presentation, a lower value is better, as it represents a shorter lag to initial profitability. The solid line at the bottom of Figure 7.3 represents cases that report 12 or more start-up activities. If this occurs within the first three months, the average time to initial profitability is about four months. If this takes 25–36 months to occur, the average time to profitability is about 14 months.

In contrast, the top dashed line represents efforts that report up to three start-up activities. If this occurs in the first month, the average time to profitability is about 18 months. If this takes 13 or more months, the average time to profitability is over 36 months or three years. So the shortest average time to profitability, four months, is for nascent ventures that implement 12 or more activities within three months, and the longest, 36 months, is for nascent ventures that take more than 12 months to implement three start-up activities, or twelve times longer.

The sooner more start-up activities are implemented, the sooner nascent ventures reach profitability.

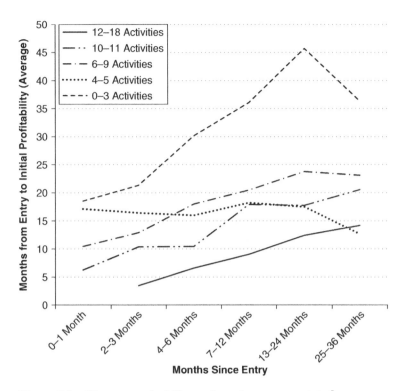

Figure 7.3   Time to profitability and total start-up activity[5]

A similar assessment of nascent ventures that were abandoned, or quit, is provided in Figure 7.4. Those that report three or fewer activities, the dashed line at the top, take the longest to disengage, from two to three years. These ventures may not be receiving a lot of attention.

Those ventures implementing ten or more start-up activities, the two lines at the bottom of the first three months in Figure 7.4, reflect a striking shift over time. If their start-up activities occur within the first three months they disengage, on average, within 15 months. If it takes over a year to implement ten or more start-up activities, disengagement takes, on average, 24 months or longer. This suggests that more start-up activity reduces the time required to determine whether a business idea can be profitable. But more complicated or involved initiatives may require longer to implement start-up activities and delay a decision to disengage.

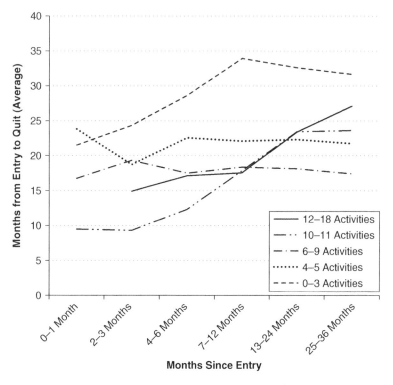

Figure 7.4   Time to quit and total start-up activity[6]

OVERVIEW

This attention to the start-up activities suggests:

- A wide range of activities are involved in business creation; the timing and mix of activities varies dramatically across nascent ventures.
- It takes longer, on average, to abandon a start-up than to reach initial profitability.
- The more activities initiated early in the start-up process the sooner the nascent venture will reach initial profitability.
- There is great diversity in the time required to abandon a nascent venture; very active start-up teams may abandon ventures quickly, minimizing the sunk costs.

Start-up activities are important indicators that a nascent entrepreneurial team is making progress on implementing a new firm. But more complicated and innovative ventures may take longer to organize and implement, so a careful assessment of the potential for the venture should accompany a review of start-up activity progress.

POLICY IMPLICATIONS

Programs designed to encourage entry into business creation should provide realistic information about the amount of time required to reach an outcome, particularly the wide variation in the time it takes to reach profitability and the benefits of accelerating the schedule of start-up activity.

These descriptions are based on typical nascent ventures that will compete in established sectors. The results suggest that policies and programs to encourage established business creation be designed for a range of start-up periods. While some nascent ventures reach profitability in several months, it may take several years, or many months after formal registration, for some nascent ventures to reach profitability. Programs and policies that expect results in a shorter period may encourage a premature disengagement, before the venture can be profitable. Careful case-by-case assessments can be justified.

NOTES

1. These were identified as both significant and had potential for harmonization across five different PSED studies. There were 66 activities across all cohorts, the largest (U.S. PED II) included 51 (Reynolds, Hechavarria, Tian, Samuelsson, and Davidsson, 2016, Table 4).
2. Based on activity in the first 72 months among nascent ventures in the U.S. PSED I and II cohorts of nascent entrepreneurs from the five-cohort data file (Reynolds, Hechavarria, Tian, Samuelsson, and Davidsson, 2016). Weights adjusted to compensate for bias is sampling, start-up team size, and duration in the start-up process (n=1,418).
3. See note to Figure 7.1.
4. See note to Figure 7.1. Two activities, excluding serious thought, are the criteria for entry into the start-up process.
5. See note to Figure 7.1, 507 cases.
6. See note to Figure 7.1, 687 cases.

8. Some activities are more helpful than others

Asked about the major problems they confront, entrepreneurs respond as follows:

> Early on it was hard for Jason to get partners or investors to take his internet business seriously.[1]

> Getting permits and approvals to provide fuel service for Hobart's River Marina has taken some time. The main supplier is a Caribbean oil company and they operate on different timetables.[2]

> There is a lack of capital to promote wooden pens for deer and moose. A human-interest television news show on Pens and Puzzles had a spot that improved Christmas sales.[3]

> I found a place for a Ralph's Pretty Good Groceries and got some people to help fix it up but after 3 weeks they never came back; then there were problems with the electricity.[4]

> Martin started by getting a business license for his publishing company. Then he started getting calls before he was ready to deliver the product. Martin is now trying to complete the first project so he can accept new clients.[5]

> Margaret is still working full-time and starting a bee keeping operation was demanding more money and time than she expected; it is hard to grow the business when you are short on resources.[6]

When asked about their major challenges, almost two-fifths (38%) of the nascent entrepreneurs mention operational issues and a third (33%) mention obtaining financial support, as shown in Table 8.1. Third on the list is attracting customers, which includes dealing effectively with the competition, mentioned by one quarter (26%). Only one in 33 (3%) expect personal or family issues as a major complication at the beginning of the process. None mentions the potential attraction of other career opportunities. The overwhelming focus is on problems related to establishing the nascent venture.

Table 8.1   Problems expected by nascent entrepreneurs[7]

Issue/Problem	Anticipated by All Nascent Entrepreneurs (%)
Operational issues	38.3
Obtaining financial support	32.7
Attracting customers, income	26.0
Personal, family issues	3.0
	100.0

The major problems mentioned by those that have quit are very different. Table 8.2 compares the responses of the individuals when they began the start-up and when they disengaged. These are responses for the same group of nascent entrepreneurs at the beginning and end of the process. Two types of issues emerge: those related to the business and those related to personal issues.

Table 8.2   Discontinued nascent ventures: problems expected and reasons for quitting[8]

Issue/Problem	Anticipated by Nascent Entrepreneurs that Quit (%)	Reported Reason for Quitting (%)
Operational issues	39.4	13.5
Attracting customers, income	29.3	31.8
Obtaining financial support	28.5	15.3
Personal, family issues	2.8	30.0
Other career opportunities		9.4
	100.0	100.0

Three in five mention complications with the business that have led to the shutdown, of which one-third (32%) mention attracting customers or revenue. Obtaining financial support and operational complications are each mentioned by about one in six (15%) as a major reason for quitting. The importance given to attracting customers shifts dramatically from entering the process to the exit.

It is ranked third by all nascent entrepreneurs in Table 8.1 and in second place by those that quit at the beginning of the process in Table 8.2. Yet it is the primary complication mentioned by those that quit in Table 8.2. This may reflect a failure to recognize the importance associated with attracting customers when they entered the start-up process. It could, however, indicate that the financial and operational issues were resolved early in the start-up process, so that the next problem for attention was attracting customers and income.

For two in five of the discontinued ventures, the major complications are personal or family issues (30%), such as a need to care for a relative or returning to school, or the attraction of other career options (9%). In contrast, only 3% mentioned any such issues as a complication as they entered the start-up process. These personal and family complications appear to gain prominence as business creation is pursued.

Most nascent entrepreneurs do not seem to be aware of the significance of attracting customers and managing family and personal issues as they enter the start-up process.

START-UP ACTIVITIES AND OUTCOMES

Starting a business involves a full set of challenges. Responses are reflected in the start-up activities initiated by the entrepreneurial team, discussed in Chapter 7. Knowing which activities are more likely to facilitate a successful outcome could serve as a guide for entrepreneurs confronting choices for emphasis; it is difficult to do everything at once.

Eighteen of these activities were discussed in Chapter 7. It is awkward, however, to pursue an assessment of each activity, particularly since they are often initiated together. It turns out that these activities tend to occur in clusters. Each cluster is a set of activities that are initiated together. The six clusters are:

- *Public presence* for the nascent venture such as any promotion, initial sales, phone or website listing, or registration with a government agency.[9]
- *Operation* of business activity such as producing goods or services, initiating supplier credit, or an owner working full-time for the venture.[10]

- Creating an *infrastructure* by acquiring physical assets like buildings or machinery, assembling parts, supplies, or inventory, or financial investments by the owners.[11]
- *Planning* efforts such as financial projections, defining markets, or preparation of a business plan.[12]
- *Funding* related efforts such as applying for financial support or obtaining external funds.[13]
- Creating a more *complex* effort by organizing a start-up team and applying for legal recognition of intellectual property such as patents, copyrights, or trademarks.[14]

These clusters, in turn, can be considered in relationship to success at achieving initial profitability.

This is illustrated in Figure 8.1, which shows the relationship between emphasis on the different clusters of activities in the first 24 months and the final outcomes. Comparisons of emphasis on different clusters is facilitated by standardizing differences from the average values.

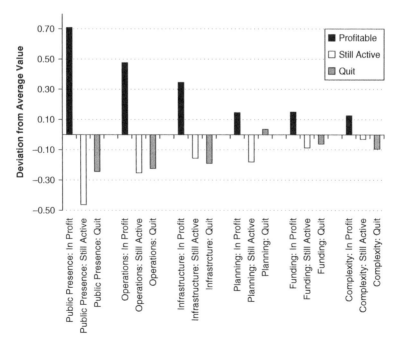

Figure 8.1   Activity domains and outcomes[15]

The clusters are organized, from left to right, in terms of the difference in emphasis between those ventures that reach profitability (black bar) and those that quit (grey bar). All six differences are highly statistically significant. It is clear the biggest difference is associated with developing a public presence for the business. Those that achieve initial profitability give much more emphasis to making the new business visible than those that quit. Those initiatives still active in the start-up mode are like those that quit. The activity cluster with the second greatest impact is implementing a production process, closely followed by creating the business infrastructure or a physical presence for the operation. There is much less of an impact for two activity clusters that receive a lot of attention: business planning and external fundraising. Considered as an independent factor, activities reflecting a more complex undertaking do not have a strong substantive association with outcomes.

A great deal of emphasis has been placed on business planning, which encompasses a wide range of activities, from verbal descriptions of a business idea to detailed plans including multi-year financial projections. Compelling evidence that business planning facilitates the creation of profitable businesses has yet to be developed.[16] As shown in Figure 8.1, those ventures that reach profitability have given more attention to planning than those that quit or continue to be active in the startup process. While this positive association is statistically significant, other activities may be more helpful in achieving profitability.

A business plan represents a strategy for coordinating physical, financial, and human resources to provide goods and services. These other activities—contacting customers, working on procedures to deliver a good or service, and putting a productive operation in place—all involve assembling information that may affect a business plan. In some cases the adjustments might be dramatic, leading to major shifts in promotions, production planning, or pricing strategies. While some attention to planning would seem necessary for effective business development, an early emphasis on customers and operational issues would seem to be the most useful for achieving profitability.

Two significant features of the start-up process are the outcome and the time to reach an outcome. A shorter time to initial profitability is associated with an early emphasis on developing a public presence, implementing operations, creating an infrastructure, and planning.[17] This would reduce the sunk cost, or investment, required to implement a new firm.

MULTIPLE ACTIVITY CLUSTERS AND OUTCOMES

In most cases, more than one cluster of activities is pursued at the same time. A team may be working on procedures to deliver a product at the same time as they are developing a marketing campaign and seeking outside financial support. It is not always clear which sets of activity clusters might be the most critical for reaching initial profitability. One analysis allows comparisons of different combinations of start-up activities to identify which combination has the greatest impact on the outcome. Once the most influential combination is identified, the analysis locates the second most influential combination of start-up activities. This continues for the third, fourth, and so on. Categories of nascent ventures with different emphases on two activity clusters in the first 24 months are compared in terms of outcomes after 72 months in Figure 8.2.

For these nascent ventures, the extent to which the start-up team is providing a pubic presence for the nascent venture is identified as having the greatest effect on the outcome. The secondary emphasis varies somewhat, depending on the amount of emphasis given to emphasizing a public presence. The result is 12 categories, identified by different pairs of start-up activity clusters. The joint emphasis is provided in the group labels, and the proportion of all cases in each group is indicated in parentheses. They are ordered in terms of the proportion that reach profitability.

Diversity in achieving profitability is dramatic. Over three-fourths (79% and 78%) of the most profitable groups (A, B) reach profitability compared to one in 25 (4%) of the least successful group (L). Group A nascent ventures are 20 times more likely to reach profitability than group L nascent ventures.

The groups A and B nascent teams have given strong emphasis to providing a public presence for the venture (initial promotions, registration, website, or initial sales) and are involved in a more complex endeavor that involves a start-up team or application for intellectual property rights (A) or emphasizing getting the operation in place (B).

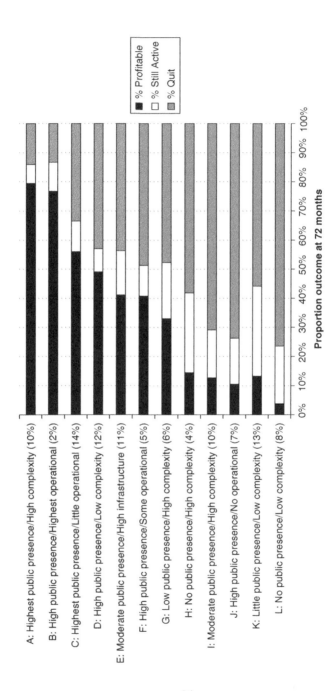

Figure 8.2   Multiple start-up activity domains and outcomes[18]

Half or more of the nascent ventures in the next two groups (C and D) reach profitability, again reflecting an emphasis on creating a public presence for the new business. The next three groups (E, F, and G) have a reduced emphasis on a public presence and about one-third reach profitability.

The next four groups (H, I, J, and K) either have much less emphasis on a public presence (H, I, and K) or have promoted a business with little operational capability (J). About one tenth have reached profitability and over half have disengaged from the start-up process. Start-up teams in the final group (L) appear to have done very little to implement a new firm and three-fourths have disengaged.

The top two groups (A, B) are 12% of the nascent ventures but provide 26% of the profitable ventures. The next two (C, D) are 25% of the nascent ventures and the source of 37% of profitable new firms. Taken together, these four groups represent one-quarter (25%) of the nascent ventures but lead to 63% of the profitable firms.

Considering that six different clusters of activities were identified, it is of interest that only four—related to public presence, complexity, implementing infrastructure or operations—are included as affecting profitability. Activity related to planning efforts or developing external financing were not identified as having, either on their own or in conjunction with other activity clusters, a significant impact on the outcomes. This is not evidence that they are not relevant, only that other activities pursued in the first 24 months seems to have greater influence.

OVERVIEW

Starting any nascent venture involves confronting a unique set of problems. Nascent entrepreneurs often focus on the immediate issues that arise. It would seem that the challenges expected at the start of the process are not always the ones that lead to disengagement.

Some issues, however, are more urgent that others and not everything can be done at once. Choices must be made about allocating time, money, and building credibility in the business community. In general, an early emphasis on understanding the interests of the customers, creating a system for delivering goods and services, and developing a business infrastructure seems to facilitate profitability and may shorten the time to reach profitability. This implication is consistent with the focus of the "lean start-up" strategy, which encourages efforts to create new products and services to focus on "customer discovery."[19] It has been adopted as the focus of the National Science Foundation sponsored I-Corp (Innovation Corp) training for commercializing scientific advances.[20]

This does not suggest that developing a business plan or seeking financial support are not important, but both will be affected in major ways by the information developed as other issues are resolved.

Equally important, the time required to determine if the business idea is viable may be shorter the sooner the public presence, organizational systems, and administrative infrastructure are established.

POLICY IMPLICATIONS

There is robust evidence that programs and seminars designed to facilitate successful business should emphasize the development of a public presence for the venture and in determining how to satisfy customer needs. Attention to developing an effective operation, including access to an appropriate infrastructure may also expedite reaching profitability. While issues related to funding and developing explicit plans are valuable, they should not be the primary focus of training and mentoring initiatives.

NOTES

1. PSED RESPID 337800081, fictitious name.
2. PSED RESPID 328100545, fictitious name.
3. PSED RESPID 328100515, fictitious name.
4. PSED RESPID 328100173, fictitious name.
5. PSED RESPID 328100173, fictitious name.
6. PSED RESPID 328100210, fictitious name.
7. Based on PSED II items AA6A. Case weights adjusted to compensate for bias in sampling, start-up team size, and duration in the process (n=804).
8. Based on PSED II items AA6A and BE52, CE52, DE52, EE52, and FE52. Case weights adjusted to compensate for bias in sampling, start-up team size, and duration in the process (n=418).
9. This four-item index includes initiation of business registration, promotion of products or services, public phone listing or website, or initial sales or income. Cronbach's Alpha is 0.56.
10. This three-item index includes hiring employees, initiation of supplier credit, and full-time commitment to the start-up initiative. Cronbach's Alpha is 0.49.
11. This three-item index includes leasing or purchase of major assets; purchase of

materials, supplies, or parts; or entrepreneur investment of their own money. Cronbach's Alpha is 0.50.

12. This three-item index includes initiation of business planning, development of financial projections, and defining markers. Cronbach's Alpha is 0.49.

13. This two-item index includes asking for funding and receiving external financial support. Cronbach's Alpha is 0.67.

14. This two item index includes the organization of a start-up team and initiating applications for a patent, copyright, or trademark. Cronbach's alpha is 0.24.

15. Activity clusters based on assessment in Reynolds (2016) (n=1,418). This result varies from Reynolds (2016, Figure 8.1) in that activity clusters are measured in first 24 months but all cases with outcomes are included with weights adjusted to compensate for bias in sampling, start-up team size, and duration in the process. All six differences are statistically significant at the 0.000 level.

16. A commentary on the lack of agreement on the impact of business planning is provided in Reynolds (2016, pp. 12–14).

17. Based on all cases (n=341) that reached initial profitability with weights adjusted to compensate for bias in sampling, start-up team size, and duration in the process. All have negative correlations with a two-tailed statistical significance of 0.01 or greater.

18. Based on SPSS v24 of CHAID analysis (TREE), it utilizes the data and procedures discussed in Reynolds (2016, Chapter 8) to predict all cases reaching initial profitability from all cases with outcomes. Assessment restricted to U.S. PSED I and II cases. Case weights adjusted to account for sampling bias, start-up team size, and duration in the start-up process (n=1,333). Only firm and start-up cluster variables were entered in the assessment, omitting any control factors, such as industry sector. Based on the 12 categories, the proportion of cases still active or discontinued were determined with a crosstabs assessment.

19. Osterwalder and Pigneur (2013); Reiss (2011).

20. National Science Foundation (2016).

9.   It takes some effort

Starting a firm requires some personal investments. Start-up teams expect to invest time and money in a nascent venture before it will be profitable. While every start-up reflects a unique business idea and the social and economic context may vary widely, it is useful to consider the range of investments reported by those in the start-up process. The range of contributions of time and money is considered in relation to outcomes, followed by a discussion of factors that may affect the amount of the investments. While the amounts for individual ventures may be modest, the total annual investments for ten million start-ups being initiated by eighteen million nascent entrepreneurs in 2016 is considerable: about three and a half million work years and $200 billion.[1]

SWEAT EQUITY OR HOURS COMMITTED[2]

How much work is required to start a new firm? The average time invested in those ventures that reach profitability is about 1,500 person-hours, or 38 person-weeks of full-time work, presented in the top panel of Figure 9.1. But the distribution is very skewed. About half take less than 560 person-hours, the median value. A small proportion take considerable investments. About one in 11 (9%) absorb over 4,000 person-hours and the maximum in this cohort is 22,800 person-hours, over ten years of full-time work.

Those start-ups that are abandoned absorb an average of 770 person-hours, or 19 person-weeks of full-time effort. The median time, however, is 200 person-hours, or five person-weeks.

Those ventures that are still in the start-up phase have absorbed an average of 2,000 person-hours, or 50 person-weeks. The median, 1,000 person-hours or 25 person-weeks, is also considerably higher than those nascent ventures that have reached profitability or are abandoned.

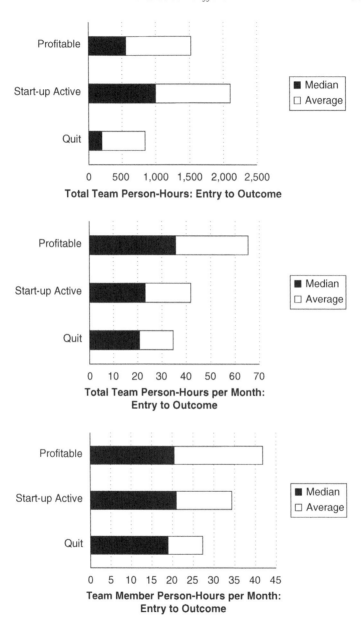

Figure 9.1 Time devoted to nascent venture by outcome

Very few start-ups receive full-time attention from a start-up team. It takes an average of 14 months to reach initial profitability. As shown in the middle panel of Figure 9.1, the average monthly team contribution is about 65 person-hours, the median is 36. Adjusting for the size of the start-up teams, and as shown in the bottom panel of Figure 9.1, this is an average of 42 hours per month per team member, a median of 20 hours per month for each team member.

Those efforts that are abandoned take slightly longer to reach an outcome: 18 months on average. The middle panel of Figure 9.1 indicates an average contribution of 35 hours per month and a median value of 21. Adjusting for team size, this is an average of 27 hours per month for each team member, or a median of 19 hours per month. While a substantial personal commitment, it is somewhat less than those on start-up teams that lead to profitable firms.

There are, finally, those nascent ventures that remain in the start-up process, at least for the duration of the data collection. As shown in the middle panel of Figure 9.1, the average monthly investment is about 43 person-hours; the median value is 23. Adjusted for team size, this is about 34 hours per month per team member, a median value of 21 hours per month.

Regardless of the final status of the nascent venture, most are not receiving full-time efforts from any one at the initial stages of the start-up process. A full-time effort would be at least 160 hours each month. This "shortfall" reflects a major feature of the work situation of most nascent entrepreneurs. The majority, about four-fifths, are working or managing another business while they pursue the new start-up venture. Full-time work on a start-up typically appears about eight months after entry into the start-up process, as shown in Figure 7.1. Full-time work on a nascent venture may be rare for those initiatives that are discontinued or in the start-up process for extended periods of time.

These average values, however, do not capture the enormous diversity in effort devoted to start-up ventures. As shown in Table 9.1 the maximum amount of time for a venture to reach profitability was 22,800 person-hours, or 11 years of full-time work. On the other hand, only one in nine that reached profitability reported over two years of full-time work. In most cases this work is shared among team members. A larger proportion, one in six, reported less than 100 hours, or two and half weeks of full-time work before reaching profitability. This is quite manageable for a

Table 9.1   Total team person-hours devoted to start-up effort[3]

	Initial Profitability	Active Start-up	Quit	All Cases
Average (Hours)	1,511	2,014	770	1,386
Median (Hours)	560	1,000	200	573
Minimum (Hours)	5	1	10	1
Max, reset (Hours)[a]	12,549	19,801	10,552	10,115
Max, original (Hours)	22,800	42,000	27,000	42,000
1–100 Hours	15.5%	25.0%	30.5%	24.2%
101–500 Hours	34.5%	11.7%	34.7%	24.4%
501–1,500 Hours	14.7%	25.8%	20.0%	21.3%
1,501–4,000 Hours	24.1%	25.0%	12.6%	21.0%
4,000–Max hours	11.2%	12.5%	2.1%	9.1%
	100.0%	100.0%	99.9%	100.0%

Note: a. Extreme cases set to mean plus 3 × standard deviation for each outcome.

single person. On the other hand, most start-up ventures are not weekend projects.

The maximum time investment among those that quit was 27,000 person-hours and one in seven (15%) involved over 1,500 person-hours. The maximum investment among those still active was about 42,000 person-hours, or 20 person-years of work. The average, 2,000 person-hours, is almost three times greater than the teams that quit, 770 person-hours, and almost two in five (38%) have invested over 1,500 person-hours. A small number of "still in process" nascent ventures absorb large investments of personal time.

At the other extreme are a substantial proportion of nascent ventures that receive little or no time commitments. Of the 15% of start-up efforts that become profitable, 30% of those that are abandoned, and 25% of those still active after six years have received no more than 100 person-hours of effort.

HOW MUCH MONEY IS INVOLVED?[4]

Future owners of new businesses contribute funds in two ways: direct investments that reflect equity ownership and loans to the new business. These contributions are combined in summarizing the total financial support provided by members of the start-up teams, presented in Table 9.2 in relation to outcome for the nascent ventures. All data from the 1999 and 2005 cohorts are inflation adjusted to 2016 values.

Start-up teams provide an average of $27,817 in 2016 dollars to those ventures that reach profitability. As with person-hours invested, the distribution is highly skewed, and the median value is much lower; half reach profitability with total investments below $7,143. But the range is considerable and skewed by some large investments. The maximum reported was almost two million ($1,720,000); which was re-set to $566,000 when computing the average. While one in eight (12%) start-up teams provided over $50,000; about one in ten (11%) involved no initial funds and about one-quarter (27%) involved less than $5,000. The majority of start-ups that reach profitability are not requiring large amounts of initial funding. These are probably not very complicated endeavors.

The diversity is just as great among those nascent ventures that were abandoned. While the average investment was $38,374, half involved less than $2,500 and one in eight (12%) received no funds before they were shut down. The maximum was over $15 million, re-set to $2,600,000 to compute the averages.

There is also a considerable range among those that remain in the start-up process. The average initial investment is $16,000, but half invest no more than $3,356. One-third (36%) have received no initial funds. While one in 12 (8%) have received at least $50,000, including one absorbing $1,655,944, the large majority have not received major investments from the start-up team. This may be one reason the future of these nascent ventures has not been resolved.

Financial investments are rarely one-time, lump sum contributions. Funds are generally provided during the start-up process, as expenses are incurred. The burn rate, or funds provided per month, is presented by outcomes in Figure 9.2.

As might be expected those that reach initial profitability receive the highest average monthly contributions, about $2,800 per month; but the median value is about $600 per month. Launching many new ventures does not involve a major cash infusion. The average monthly investments for those ventures that are discontinued is somewhat less, about $2,000 per month; but half involve less than $160 per month. Because those still active have been in the start-up process for longer periods of time, their average monthly contributions are much lower, about $350 per month, and half receive no more than $70 per month.

Table 9.2   Total team funds provided to start-up effort[5]

	Initial Profitability	Active Start-up	Quit	All Cases
Average (2016$)[a]	$27,817	$16,021	$38,374	$26,292
Median (2016$)	$7,143	$3,356	$2,519	$4,215
Minimum (2016$)	$0	$0	$0	$0
Max, Reset (2016$)[b]	$566,189	$497,650	$2,607,569	$1,948,471
Max, original (2016$)[c]	$1,720,430	$1,655,944	$15,476,190	$15,476,190
None reported	11.0%	34.8%	12.3%	17.4%
$1–1,000	5.9%	2.2%	21.0%	12.9%
$1,001–5,000	20.6%	16.7%	28.7%	23.9%
$5,001–15,000	32.4%	21.7%	15.0%	20.7%
$15,001–50,000	17.6%	16.7%	10.7%	13.8%
$50,001+	12.5%	8.0%	12.3%	11.3%
	100.0%	100.1%	100.0%	100.0%

Notes:
a. All values adjusted to 2016 dollars.
b. Extreme cases set to 3 × standard deviation for each outcome.
c. Original maximum values with no weighting adjustment.

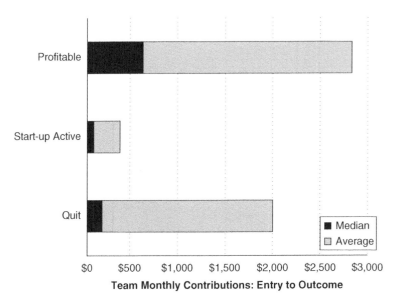

Figure 9.2   Start-up teams' monthly financial contributions by outcome

Most striking about tracking work and funds provided to nascent ventures by the start-up teams is the substantial diversity. The following reviews a range of factors that may affect these contributions.

FACTORS AFFECTING TEAM INVESTMENTS

The investments in nascent ventures during the start-up period may be affected by the nature of the venture itself or the personal background of the start-up team. Five characteristics of the venture are considered in relation to the average number of person-hours and start-up team financing invested in the initiative in Table 9.3.

Larger start-up teams appear to provide more sweat equity, hours of work, and funds for a start-up, particularly for teams of three or more. Family teams seem to reflect a much larger commitment, averaging over 4,000 hours and almost $80,000. This is approximately three times the average amount.

Growth oriented ventures seem to receive more labor input, 1,800

Table 9.3   *Venture characteristics and nascent venture investments*[6]

	Total Person-Hours for Nascent Venture (Average)	Statistical Significance	Total Funds for Venture (Average, 2016$)	Statistical Significance
All Nascent Ventures	1,387		26,292	
Start-up Team Size				
One	1,278		24,482	
Two	1,445		29,059	
Three	2,562		55,587	
Four or more	3,204	*	37,528	ns
Team Structure				
Sole proprietorship	1,233		24,520	
Spousal pair	1,090		19,488	
Family team	4,024		78,588	
Collegial team	2,086	***	29,770	ns
Growth Aspirations				
Keep size easy to manage	1,289		28,075	
Maximize growth	1,869	*	20,187	ns
Technological Emphasis				
None	1,401		25,788	
Low	1,581		29,632	
Some	1,055		14,880	
High	1,675	ns	49,199	ns
Economic Sector				
Extractive	1,373		89,544	
Transformation	1,137		29,001	
Business services	1,286		36,407	
Consumer services	1,574	ns	13,888	ns

Note: Statistical significance: ns = not significant; *=0.05; ***=0.001.

person-hours versus 1,200 for those ventures expected to be easy to manage. But they appear to receive slightly less financing ($20,000 versus $28,000).

The extent of the technological emphasis has no systematic effect on the number of person-hours invested, but those with the greatest emphasis seem to receive twice the average financial investment, $49,000 compared to $26,000.

There seems to be an economic sector effect, with ventures involved in physical transformations (construction, manufacturing, transportation, wholesale) receiving less person-hour investments. This may reflect more efficient implementation before an outcome is determined or a larger proportion of modest start-ups in construction, such as plumbers or electricians. The small proportion in the extractive sectors (farming, forestry, mining) seem to require much larger financial commitments than average ($89,000 vs $26,000).

Sole Proprietors and Contributions

Personal factors may also affect these investments. The relationship of six characteristics of single individuals pursuing sole proprietorships on contributions is summarized in Table 9.4. There are very few relationships that are either substantively or statistically significant.

Working full-time has no relationship to time invested in the nascent venture: both those with and without work invest about 1,200 person-hours. But those with full-time work while they initiate a new firm may be investing more funds, $26,000 versus $17,000, but the difference is not statistically significant.

Men and women are investing about the same amount of time, 1,200 person-hours. Men, however, appear to invest about four times as much money as women, $40,000 versus $10,000; this is clearly statistically significant. It probably reflects the requirements associated with entering different market sectors.

There is no difference in either time or funds invested associated with the age of the sole proprietor.

There are some suggestive differences associated with ethnic background. Minorities (African-Americans and Hispanics) seem to invest more time than Whites (1,500 versus 1,100 person-hours) but Whites seem to invest more funds ($28,000 versus $20,000). Neither difference is statistically significant.

Those with no prior experience with start-ups appear to invest less time and money in their new ventures compared to those with prior start-up experience. While the experienced nascent entrepreneurs are devoting two to three times as much time and money, the differences are not statistically significant.

Work experience in the same industry would seem to be associated with more time investment, but it is not statically significant. A small increase in financial contributions is not statistically significant.

Table 9.4   Sole proprietorship factors associated with nascent venture investments[7]

	Person-Hours (Average)	Statistical Significance	Funds (Average, 2016$)	Statistical Significance
All Nascent Ventures	1,233		24,520	
Working, Managing Full-Time				
Yes	1,188		26,454	
No	1,297	ns	17,252	ns
Gender Composition				
Male only	1,259		39,956	
Female Only	1,180	ns	9,575	**
Team Age Composition				
Only 18–34 years old	1,215		24,819	
Only 35 and older	1,195	ns	24,819	ns
Team Ethnic Composition				
White only	1,108		28,230	
Minority only	1,509	ns	20,526	ns
Team Start-up Experiences				
None	822		18,212	
1–3 other start-ups	1,697		29,233	
4 or more other start-ups	1,320	ns	53,119	ns
Team Start-up Industry Experience				
Up to 5 years	1,015		23,202	
6–30 years	1,384		25,963	
Over 30 years	2,305	ns	25,018	ns

Note: Statistical significance: ns = not significant; **=0.01.

Start-up Team Members and Contributions

The same factors are considered in relation to start-up teams in Table 9.5, but in this case the investment per team member is presented. There are some differences. For example, those working full-time versus not employed have the same time investments, but those not working are associated with twice as much financial contribution as those working.

Gender has a different association. In mixed gender teams, most are pairs of spouses, and have the lowest investments of time and money.

Table 9.5 *Team member factors associated with nascent venture investments*[8]

	Person-Hours per Team Members (Average)	Statistical Significance	Funds per Team Members (Average, 2016$)	Statistical Significance
All Nascent Ventures	1,726		31,887	
Working, Managing Full-Time				
Yes	1,745		26,928	
No	1,686	ns	52,030	ns
Gender Composition				
Male only	2,005		40,667	
Mixed	1,532		24,336	
Female Only	2,119	ns	57,580	ns
Team Age Composition				
Only 18–34 years old	1,721		32,336	
Both 18–34 and 35 and older	1,675		43,370	
Only 35 and older	1,760	ns	24,245	ns
Team Ethnic Composition				
White only	1,674		36,318	
White and minority	1,698		40,454	
Minority only	2,117	ns	15,215	ns
Team Start-up Experiences				
None	1,508		16,305	
1–3 other start-ups	1,257		35,743	
4 or more other start-ups	3,389	***	56,235	ns
Team Start-up Industry Experience				
Up to 5 years	1,170		29,631	
6–30 years	1,962		28,755	
Over 30 years	2,250	ns	50,577	ns

Note: Statistical significance: ns = not significant; ***=0.001.

While those on teams of men and women invest about the same amount of time, the per member financial investments of women team members appear somewhat higher ($57,580). This is in sharp contrast to women involved as sole practitioners, who invest much less ($9,575).

There is no systematic relationship between the age distribution among team members and their contributions.

The ethnic composition of the teams has little apparent effect on per member time contributions, although it may be slightly higher for minority only teams. But minority only teams seem to invest about half as much money in start-ups ($15,000) compared to White only or White and Minority start-up teams ($36,000 to $40,000).

Previous start-up experience seems to be associated with both time and money commitments. Those teams with four or more prior start-ups lead to over twice as much per team member time commitment (3,400 versus less than 1,600) and, compared to those with no prior experience, over three times the per member financial commitment ($56,000 versus $16,000).

More than five years of same industry experience among the team members is associated with a 50% increase in per member time investment: 1,800 versus 1,200 person-hours. Teams with over 30 years of same industry experience have almost twice the per member financial investment ($50,000 versus $29,000).

OVERVIEW

A review of the time and money invested in nascent ventures by start-up teams makes clear that:

- The typical start-up investment involves 1,400 person-hours of time and $26,000 of funds.
- There is enormous diversity in these personal investments. This probably reflects diversity in aspirations, business plan complexity, and variation in the resources and experience available to the start-up team.
- The amount of effort varies from several weeks to many years of full-time effort. Nine months of full-time work is typical for those ventures that reach profitability, spread over 13 months. Those that are discontinued absorb about five months of work, spread over 18 months. Those still active in the start-up

process report almost a year of full-time work, spread over four years.

- Diversity in personal financial support from the start-up teams is even greater, from nothing to millions. About half of all nascent ventures have absorbed less than $5,000; about 10% more than $50,000. The average contributions to those that are profitable is $28,000, $38,000 for those abandoned, and about $16,000 for those that remain active in the start-up process.
- While ventures initiated by start-up teams appear to receive greater investments of time and money, the effects of growth aspirations, technological sophistication, and economic sector on start-up investments is modest.
- While previous experience with start-up ventures and same sector work experience is associated with greater investments in a nascent venture, other personal factors such as gender, age, and ethnicity have modest or inconsistent association with nascent venture investments.
- Individuals involved in team efforts tend to invest, on average, about as much time and money into nascent ventures as those developing sole proprietorships. The total investments in team efforts is, therefore, somewhat greater. This may account for their greater success in reaching profitability.

This overview has provided information on the range of team investments involved in business creation. It does indicate the range of investments of time and money a start-up team can expect in the business creation process.

POLICY RELEVANCE

The total amount of time and money devoted by 17,800,000 nascent entrepreneurs to 9,500,000 U.S. nascent ventures in 2016 is substantial. In one year about 3.4 million work years and $194 billion in funds were invested by start-up teams. A substantial proportion of these contributions are committed to ventures that do not achieve profitability. Figure 9.3 shows the amounts provided to nascent ventures with different outcomes.

Those teams that develop profitable businesses contribute 51% of the time and 34% of the total investments in nascent ventures. These

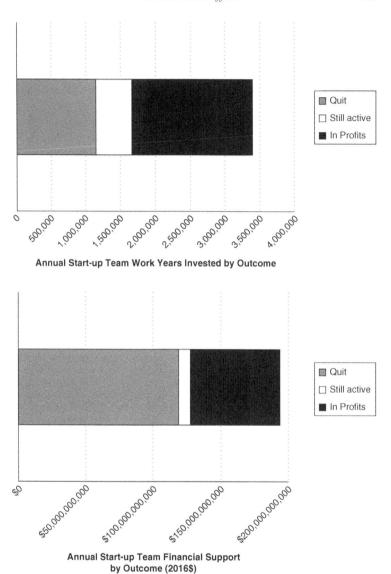

Figure 9.3   *Annual start-up team time and financial contributions:*
U.S. totals[9]

teams will receive all the benefits associated with new firm creation. In contrast, teams associated with ventures that are abandoned or continue in the start-up mode provide 49% of the work and 66% of the funds invested in business creation. These nascent entrepreneurs, however, receive none of the benefits associated with the entrepreneurial process.

There will be a substantial societal payoff if the proportion of nascent ventures that achieve profitability can be increased. In terms of policy impact, this may be considered low hanging fruit. As only two-fifths of nascent ventures achieve profitability, a slight improvement in success, from 40% to 50%, would have a substantial impact on shifting the ratio of benefits to costs by reducing the proportion of nascent ventures that do not reach profitability. This may be done by improving the proportion of nascent ventures that reach profitability or identifying those likely to quit early in the start-up process.

NOTES

1. As presented in Figure 9.3, later in the chapter.
2. All data on hours of work committed to nascent ventures taken from the four waves of the PSED I data set. The hours committed by each team member up to the date of interview is computed. The data from the wave preceding the transition to profitability or disengagement is considered the most accurate measure of total hours committed. Data from the last interview completed for those not reporting a transition to profitability or quitting is used for the "still active" cases. Extreme values are reset to three standard deviations above the average for each outcome. Cases with no data or zero hours invested are omitted from calculations. Weights adjusted for bias in sampling, start-up team size, and duration in the process are re-centered for each outcome.
3. PSED I cases reporting no time investment omitted. Venture weights adjusted for bias in sampling, start-up team size, and duration in the process and then re-centered to equal one for each outcome. Weights for all cases reflect proportion with each outcome. Initial profitability, n=116; active start-up, n=120: quit n=95: and all cases, n=331.
4. All data on personal financial commitments to nascent ventures taken from the six waves of the PSED II data set. The funds committed by each team member up to the date of each interview is computed to create a total for the venture. These totals are adjusted by year using the consumer price index (U.S. Census, U.S. Department of Commerce, no date) to create values in 2016 dollars. The sum from the wave preceding the transition to profitability or disengagement is considered the most accurate measure of total financial commitment before the outcome transition. Data from the last interview completed for those not reporting a transition to profitability or quitting is used for the "still active" cases. Extreme values are reset to the mean plus three standard deviations for each outcome. Cases with

no financial investments are included in all assessments. Weights adjusted for bias in sampling, start-up team size, and duration in the process are re-centered for each outcome.

5. PSED II venture weights adjusted for bias in sampling, start-up team size, and duration in the process and re-centered to equal one for each outcome. Weights for all cases reflect proportion with each outcome. Profitability, n=137; active start-up, n=138; quit, n=300; and all cases, n=585.

6. Time contributions based on U.S. PSED I cases with a known outcome (n=327 to 335). Financial contributions based on U.S. PSED II cases with a known outcome, all figures adjusted for inflation to equal 2016 values (n=582 to 584). In both cases weights are adjusted to account for bias in sampling, start-up team-size, and duration in the start-up process.

7. Time contributions based on U.S. PSED I cases with a known outcome (n=231). Financial contributions based on U.S. PSED II cases with a known outcome, all figures adjusted for inflation to equal 2016 values (n=436 to 444). In both cases weights are adjusted to account for bias in sampling, start-up team-size, and duration in the start-up process.

8. Time contributions based on U.S. PSED I cases with a known outcome (n=104). Financial contributions based on U.S. PSED II cases with a known outcome, all figures adjusted for inflation to equal 2016 values (n=141). In both cases weights are adjusted to account for bias in sampling, start-up team-size, and duration in the start-up process.

9. National estimates are based on U.S. Census estimate of the total population for 2016 of 323,127,513 and using estimates from 2015 that 62.2% are between 18 and 64 years of age (U.S. Census, U.S. Department of Commerce, no date). The average prevalence of nascent entrepreneurs from the annual Global Entrepreneurship Monitor (GEM) surveys from 2012 to 2016 is 8.86/100 adults 18–64 years of age (Reynolds and Hechavarria, 2016; Kelley, Singer, and Herrington, 2016; Global Entrepreneurship Research Association, 2017). The average number of owners for each enterprise from the GEM surveys from 2012 to 2014 is 1.8743 (Reynolds and Hechavarria, 2016). The results is a nascent venture prevalence rate of 4.727/100 adults 18–64 years old. This leads to an estimate of 17,807,299 nascent entrepreneurs working with 9,500,773 nascent ventures in 2016. The average values associated with the investments of time and money for the three outcomes are adjusted to annual values by correcting for the time in the start-up process for each outcome: 34 months for those reaching profitability, 37 months for those that quit, and 78 months for those still active. A preliminary version of this assessment appeared in Reynolds and Curtin (2009a, Figure 7.11).

10. Money may be necessary, but is not sufficient

Money doesn't start businesses, people do. But people often need money for two things to complete the start-up process. The first are the living expenses of the start-up team; everybody needs to eat and a place to sleep. The second is for resources to implement the new venture. There is substantial variation in both the amount of funds required and when financial support is needed during the start-up process. There are, of course, a wide range of solutions developed for these challenges. New solutions for acquiring financing are constantly being invented—internet based crowdsourcing being one of the more recent.[1]

The major strategy for covering living expenses is to continue working while developing the new business. More than four in five nascent entrepreneurs are working or managing another business while they develop the new venture. The importance of attending to their day jobs is reflected by how long it takes to begin devoting full-time to the start-up initiative. As shown in Figure 7.1, for about two-fifths (41%) full-time attention generally occurs about eight months after beginning the business creation process. Others may have working spouses, be living with parents or relatives or, for older nascent entrepreneurs, relying on retirement income.

Funding for start-up initiatives can take two forms. Informal financial support are those funds provided for the venture either directly by the start-up team or from others through a member of the start-up team. For example, a relative may loan money to a nascent entrepreneur for the start-up effort. Formal financial support is only possible after the start-up is registered as a legal entity. Only then can the venture be part of a binding contract related to financial matters, such as leasing a vehicle. Three different activities are related to the form of financial support: the initial informal contributions, the legal registration of the firm, and the initiation of formal financial support.

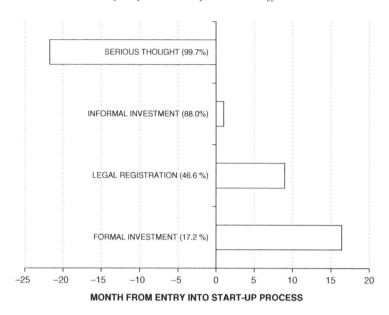

Figure 10.1   Timing of financial support events in the start-up process[2]

The timing of these events, in relation to entry into the start-up process, is presented in Figure 10.1. The initiation of serious thought, a useful reference, is reported by virtually all nascent entrepreneurs and occurs, on average, about two years before beginning business creation. The first informal investments are reported by 88% and typically occurs during the first month. For slightly less than half (47%) legal registration occurs about nine months later. Obtaining formal financial support for the nascent venture is reported by 17%. The first formal funding is received about seven months after legal registration or 16 months after starting the process.

There are major differences in both the amounts and structure of financial support before and after the venture becomes a legal entity. The following explores these differences and the relationship to outcomes.

INFORMAL FINANCIAL SUPPORT

There are two major sources of funds before the venture is a legal entity, personal savings accumulated by the start-up team and personal loans to the start-up team members. A summary, adjusted for inflation to 2016 dollars, is provided in Table 10.1. As shown in the first column, about $44,000 is provided in informal funds to the typical venture. About $28,000, or two-thirds, in the form of equity or ownership investments, and the rest, about $16,000, as loans from the members of the start-up team to the nascent venture.

One-sixth of the nascent ventures, however, do not receive any financial support. About 84% receive informal funding, and the average for these ventures is $52,000. These ventures receive about $34,000 in equity or ownership investments. But only one-third

Table 10.1   Sources and amounts of informal financial support[3]

	Average All Cases ($)	Reporting Support (%)	Average Reporting Support ($)
Total pre-legal Form Funding	43,944	84.4	52,054
Equity investments from start-up team	28,355	84.4	33,588
Debt that must be paid back	15,589	31.6	49,347
Sources of Funding			
Personal savings of start-up team	22,541	81.8	27,563
Start-up Team Member Loans to Business	6,316	23.4	27,041
Personal Loans to Start-up Team Member			
Total from all sources	16,225	23.6	68,599
Loans from family members	5,385	19.5	27,581
Loans from friends, employers, and colleagues	3,256	4.6	70,863
Loans based on personal credit cards	840	10.3	7,992
Loans from banks, financial institutions	6,209	7.2	86,314
Loans backed by assets (i.e. second mortgages)	5,616	5.7	98,098
Loans from other sources	302	0.5	61,225

(32%) receive support in the form of loans that must be paid back, which average $49,000, three times the overall average of $16,000. The single largest source of these funds are the savings of the start-up team members, which is about $22,000 for all cases and $28,000 for the 82% of cases where personal savings have been provided. Presumably the start-up team is providing cash for the other 20% from ongoing revenue, salaries or other sources.

The second major source are loans provided to members of the start-up team by various entities. The average across all ventures is about $16,000. But such loans are only provided for 24% of the start-up teams, and the average for those receiving personal loans is $69,000, over four times the average for all start-ups.

There are two major sources of these loans: personal relationships and financial institutions. The most common source are family members, provided in 20% of the cases with an average of $28,000. Friends, employers, and colleagues are a source in 5% of the cases, but the average is rather high, about $71,000.

The other major source, financial institutions, provides loans through credit cards (10%), personal loans (7%) or asset backed loans (6%). Asset backed loans reflect willingness of start-up team members to pledge personal property, such as a home or vehicle. While the proportion receiving bank support may be small, the size of the loans can be substantial, with an average of $86,000 for personal loans and $98,000 for asset backed loans. Personal credit card debt is modest, averaging $8,000.

The variation in all forms of financial support is enormous. The total informal support varies from none to $16 million, which includes one case with $3.7 million in start-up team equity. These highly skewed, or lopsided, distributions complicate assessments. Six categories of total informal support, debt (or loans) plus equity, is presented in relation to outcomes in Figure 10.2. While 16% report no informal financial support, 11% report less than $1,000. In total, then, one in four nascent ventures receive less than $1,000. About half, 52%, have from $1,000 to $25,000 in informal funding. About one in nine (12%) have from $25,000 to $90,000, and 9% report over $90,000. The largest informal or pre-registration support is $16 million.

The relationship of the amount of informal financing to the outcomes in Figure 10.2 indicates that more money is not a sure path to initial profitability. Those least likely to reach profitability, from

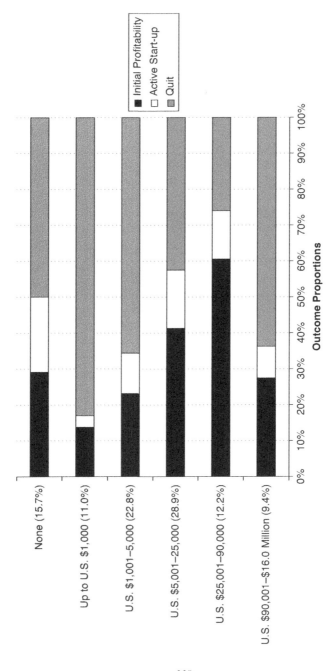

Figure 10.2   Total informal financial support and outcomes[4]

14% to 23%, are those with from $1 to $5,000 in informal funding. About 30% of those with no informal funding or over $90,000 reach initial profitability. From 40% to 60% of those ventures with $5,000 to $90,000 reach initial profitability, the highest of these groups.

The best financed ventures, those with over $90,000 in informal funds, may be distinctive. These may be more complex and innovative business ideas that take longer to develop. Slightly less than a tenth (9%) are still in the start-up phase. On the other hand, almost two-thirds (54%) have disengaged from the initiative. For these ventures, profitability may be delayed or the start-up team has rather quickly determined that the venture has no future.

This assessment makes clear, and it is confirmed by the following review of formal financial support, that money alone is not sufficient for reaching initial profitability.

FORMAL FINANCIAL SUPPORT

Slightly less than half of the nascent ventures (47%) become a legal entity in the start-up process. These ventures can enter into contracts for financial support, mostly in the form of loans that must be repaid. The total amount of support for these ventures is summarized in Table 10.2. This includes all informal, pre-legal registration contributions of both debt and equity. Formal financial support is identified in the year immediately following legal registration of the venture. Additional support in subsequent years is not included.[5]

The average for all legally registered ventures is $149,000. The average for the 99% reporting some form of financial support is only slightly higher at $150,000. About one-third (37%) of the support is in the form of equity investments before and after becoming a legal venture, which averages $58,000. The remainder is debt owed by the venture to the start-up teams as individuals, which averages $23,000, or by the venture to other sources, which averages $67,000.

Almost all of these nascent ventures (83%) received equity investments before they became legal firms, which averaged $41,000. The largest equity investments were for the 25% that received additional funds after they were legally registered, which averaged $68,000.

Informal, or pre-legal registration, debt financing was provided to 29% of these start-ups in the form of loans from members of the

Table 10.2   Sources and amounts of formal financial support[6]

	Average All Cases ($)	Reporting Support (%)	Average Reporting Support ($)
Informal and Formal Financial Support			
Total financial support	149,283	98.5	150,498
Equity investments	57,900	85.2	67,952
Debt	90,383	85.1	105,787
Timing of Equity			
Pre-formal registration	41,239	83.1	49,607
After formal registration	16,661	24.5	67,990
Timing of Debt			
Pre-formal registration, loans from the start-up team	23,087	28.8	80,254
After formal registration, loans to the venture	67,296	84.4	79,282
Sources of Nascent Venture Loans			
Bank Loans: Four Types	38,505	29.4	48,125
Asset backed loans	21,946	8.0	38,046
Government guaranteed loans	8,615	24.0	11,615
Line of credit/working capital	6,299	11.2	10,232
Other bank loans	1,645	0.9	3,232
Loans from Persons: Five Types	21,980	25.6	28,971
Personal loans from owner 1	8,615	24.0	11,614
Personal loans from owners 2–6	12,032	4.6	21,800
Personal loans from family, relatives of owners	736	2.8	1,378
Personal loans from employees	27	0.2	53
Personal loans from other individuals	570	1.9	1,088
Lease obligation debts	3,331	9.9	5,570
Supplier credit	2,049	9.1	3,415
Loans on venture sponsored credit cards	1,096	8.5	1,853
Loans from venture capital firms	67	0.1	133
Other government agency loans	–	0.1	–
Any other source	268	1.8	513

start-up teams. The average was $23,000, but after they were legal entities, 84% received loans with an average value of $79,000.

Banks were the first major source of post-legal registration loans, providing loans for 29% that averaged $48,000. For 24% the loans were guaranteed by a government entity, averaging $12,000, and 11% received a line of credit or working capital, averaging $10,000. For 8% loans from banks were provided when assets were used as collateral, averaging $38,000. About 1% received bank loans in another format, which averaged $3,000.

Personal loans are the second major source. About 24% of the ventures received loans from the respondent, identified as owner one, which averaged $12,000. Five percent received loans from other members of the start-up team, identified as numbers two through six, which averaged $22,000. In a small number of cases, 3%, loans to the firm were received from a family member of the start-up team, averaging less than $2,000. Small personal loans were made to a few ventures by employees or other individuals.

A minority of nascent ventures received support as lease obligation debts (10%), supplier credit (9%), or venture sponsored credit cards (9%). In most cases the obligations were less than $10,000.

As with the informal financing there is considerable variation in the total provided to legally registered ventures, presented in relationship to outcomes in Figure 10.3.

Two in-five (43%) report no more than $10,000 in the year following legal registration of the venture. Another fifth (22%) report from $10,000 to $50,000. On the other hand, one-third (35%) report more than $50,000 in total post-legal financing. This includes one in eight (13%) with $200,000 or more. Not shown are the one in 20 (5%) with $400,000 or more. The range, therefore, among registered nascent ventures is from 10% with no formal financing to 2% with a million or more. And 1% receive more than $3 million and one in 200 more than $5 million. The largest in the cohort is $48 million.

The association of formal funding with the outcomes, presented in Figure 10.3, is similar to that with informal funding, Figure 10.2. There is no clear association between the amount of funding and reaching profitability. From 30% to 40% of those ventures with the lowest, below $2,000, intermediate, from $10,000 to $50,000, and the highest, over $200,000 of financial support reach profitability. Almost two-thirds (over 60%) of those ventures with from $2,000 to $10,000 or from $50,000 to $200,000 in financial support reach profitability.

Except for the very highest level of funding, $200,000 or more, those receiving more funding are less likely to disengage. Half (49%) of those with the highest total funding, $200,000 or more, have abandoned the start-up initiative.

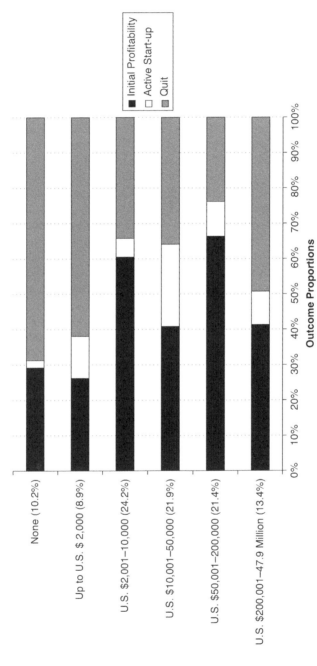

Figure 10.3   Total formal financial support and outcomes: legally registered ventures[7]

This pattern, similar to the relationship to informal funding in Figure 10.2, again suggests that start-up teams with less formal financing made an early determination that the ventures would not be profitable and quit to pursue other options. Those with high levels of formal funding were also quick to disengage once profitability was problematic.

IMPACT OF FORMAL FINANCIAL SUPPORT ON OUTCOMES

Should a start-up team make an effort to legally register a nascent venture so they can acquire formal financial support? While almost all nascent ventures receive some informal support, less than half (47%) become a legally registered venture that can receive formal funding. About one-third of this group (17%) receive formal funding in the following year. Further, the amount of formal financing varies substantially, with different effects on the outcome. It is possible to consider the effect of formal financial support on all nascent ventures, with and without formal registration.

The association between additional formal financial support on outcomes for all nascent ventures is presented in Figure 10.4. Only about one in five (20%) of all nascent ventures report any formal financial support and only one in eight (12%) more than $25,000.

One-fourth (25%) of ventures that receive no financial support reach profitability. From 60% to 80% of those that receive from $1,000 to $500,000 become profitable. Among that 1% that receive over $500,000 in formal support, about two-fifths (44%) become profitable.

Compared to those that receive no formal financial support, those that receive any funds are more likely to reach profitability.

Several features associated with formal financial support may affect this relationship. First, the preparation of a business plan and the associated financial projections may reflect a more engaged, experienced, and skilled start-up team—a team that has devoted considerable effort to identifying the customer base, organizing resources to deliver a product or service, and creating a strategy for dealing with potential competition. This could lead to a more successful outcome. Second, the money itself may facilitate implementation of a profitable venture. There is no simple way to disentangle

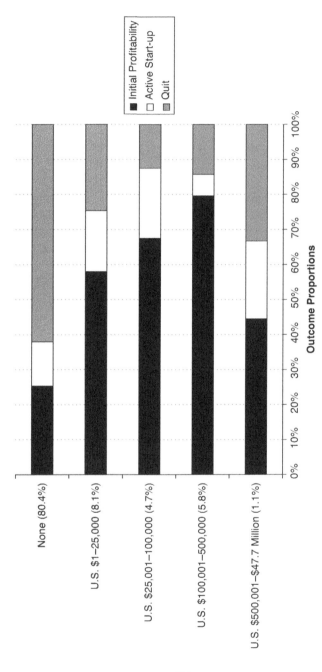

Figure 10.4 *Total formal financial support and outcomes: all nascent ventures*[8]

these two attributes of formal financing in a longitudinal panel study.

While those ventures that receive no formal financial support are less likely to reach profitability, three in four (75%) of the nascent ventures that become profitable receive less than $25,000 in formal financial support. This reflects the fact that nascent ventures with no formal support are a large majority (80%) of all start-ups. While the 20% that receive $25,000 or more in formal support are the source of one-fourth of all profitable firms, nascent ventures with little or no formal financing are a major source of profitable firms.

If a nascent team is able to convince financial institutions to provide $25,000 or more in formal financial support, they may almost triple the probability of reaching initial profitability, from 28% to 71%. This would justify the time and cost required to achieve formal legal status for the nascent venture. Successful promotion of these ventures for formal financial support probably reflects other promising features, such as an auspicious business opportunity, an experienced start-up team, and a well prepared, comprehensive business plan.

OVERVIEW

While people start businesses, financial resources are often required. Attention to the amount and sources of informal financial support before the venture is a legal agent and the formal financial support that follows legal registration suggest that:

- Informal financial support generally occurs at the very beginning of the start-up process, legal registration occurs for about half nine months later, and one-third of those legally registered get formal financing after another eight months.
- Four in five nascent ventures receive informal financial support, primarily from the start-up team, which provide about $22,000 from their personal savings.
- For about one-fourth of nascent ventures, start-up team members provide personal loans to facilitate the initiative before legal registration; the total of these loans is about $49,000.
- About half of nascent ventures become legally registered and,

in turn, able to participate in contractual relationships as a legal entity.

- Almost all (98%) nascent ventures that become legal entities receive funding, about $68,000 in equity and $106,000 in debt. There is considerable diversity among businesses: while the average was $150,000, one in ten receive nothing, a small proportion receive millions and the maximum in the cohort was $47 million.
- The major sources of formal loans to legally registered businesses are financial institutions and individuals with a relationship to a member of the start-up team.
- Nascent ventures with higher levels of formal financial support are three times as likely to become profitable as those with little or no financial support.
- A large majority of nascent ventures achieve profitability with little or no financial support.

Savvy start-up teams may be successful in obtaining financial support. Some are able to create profitable ventures without external funding. Thus: money may be necessary, but is not sufficient.

POLICY IMPLICATIONS

One of the major policy strategies to facilitate entrepreneurship is to provide financial support. While there are situations where it can be helpful, other factors will also be important. The most significant implications for public policy are:

- Providing only money for start-ups may not be an optimal strategy.
- Programs that enhance the skills and business acumen of start-up teams as well as financial support may reduce the proportion of stillborn start-ups.
- Most funded start-ups will not reach profitability. Support for a cohort of nascent firms may increase the potential for overall program success.
- Three-fourths of nascent ventures that become profitable do not receive formal funding in the early stages of the start-up process.

NOTES

1. As internet based crowdsourcing emerged after the PSED II data collection period was completed, no information on its impact is available.
2. Data from Figure 7.1.
3. Reflects a revised, updated assessment of that originally presented in Reynolds (2011a). Data is from PSED II cohort with all dollar amounts adjusted to 2016 values using consumer price index adjustments (U.S. Census, U.S. Department of Commerce, no date). Includes all cases with outcome data with case weights adjusted for bias in sampling, start-up team size, and duration in the start-up process (n=852).
4. PSED II cohort with all dollar amounts adjusted to 2016 values using consumer price index adjustments (U.S. Census, U.S. Department of Commerce, no date). Includes all cases with outcome data with case weights adjusted for bias in sampling, start-up team size, and duration in the start-up process (n=854).
5. This avoids the problem of dealing with considerable variation in the number of follow-up interviews following legal registration.
6. PSED II cohort with all dollar amounts adjusted to 2016 values using consumer price index adjustments (U.S. Census, U.S. Department of Commerce, no date). Includes all cases with outcome data with case weights adjusted for bias in sampling, start-up team size and duration in the start-up process (n=471).
7. PSED II cohort with all dollar amounts adjusted to 2016 values using consumer price index adjustments (U.S. Census, U.S. Department of Commerce, no date). Includes all cases with outcome data with case weights adjusted for bias in sampling, start-up team size, and duration in the start-up process (n=471).
8. PSED II cohort with all dollar amounts adjusted to 2016 values using consumer price index adjustments (U.S. Census, U.S. Department of Commerce, no date). Includes all cases with outcome data with case weights adjusted for bias in sampling, start-up team size, and duration in the start-up process (n=851).

11. Profits are elusive, prepare to pivot

Being a successful entrepreneur is very satisfying—that is the good news. But effective business creation often involves adjustments in the initial business idea. Some change the business plan as the venture is being implemented. More problematic is that most that enter the start-up process never reach initial profitability. When a nascent venture is abandoned, the individuals involved usually find other ways to participate in the economy. Many, to be sure, are still interested in becoming involved as nascent entrepreneurs.

PIVOT ON THE RUN: ADJUSTMENTS TO THE NASCENT VENTURE

About one in 25 (4%) report making an adjustment to the original business plan.[1] About half are considered major variations that may involve dramatic shifts in the products or services; the other half are considered minor shifts in activity. As shown in Table 11.1, almost half (47%) make changes in response to new information about customer preferences or as a reaction to the competition. About one in six (16%) mention financial issues, such as lower

Table 11.1   Reasons for business plan adjustments[2]

	(%)
Shift in demand, market conditions (e.g. competitors)	46.9
Financial: revenue, expenses, access to capital	16.3
Government regulations, other issues	10.1
Time constraints	4.1
Loss of a partner, critical employee, business contact	2.2
Miscellaneous other issues	20.3
	99.9

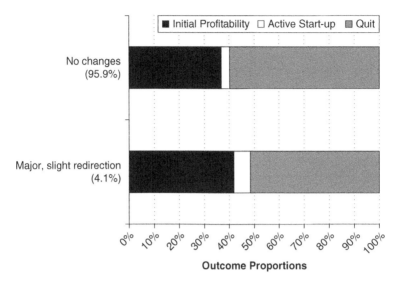

Figure 11.1   Effects of changes in nascent venture on outcomes[3]

revenue, higher expenses, or issues with access to capital. About one in ten (10%) are responding to regulations or other contextual factors. A smaller proportion mention the loss of a critical individual (partner, employee, or contact), unexpected time constraints or other issues.

Ventures that are "adjusted" may be more likely to reach profitability, as shown in Figure 11.1. About 42% of the ventures that make an adjustment reach initial profitability, compared to 37% that do not report any shifts. As a consequence, the ventures that pivot are much less likely to abandon the effort (52% versus 60%).

Overall, changes to the original business idea are uncommon, but those that do adjust, usually in response to market conditions, are more likely to reach profitability.

THE ULTIMATE PIVOT: DISENGAGEMENT

The dark side of business creation, so to speak, is that a majority of nascent ventures never become profitable. The pattern of transitions for the first six years, shown in Figure 11.2, indicate that after 72

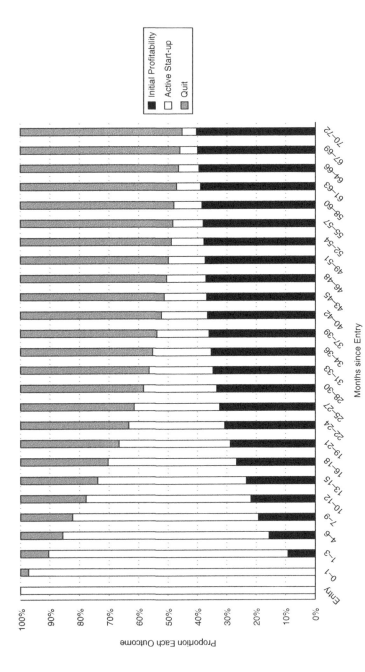

Figure 11.2   Outcome status by months since entry[4]

130

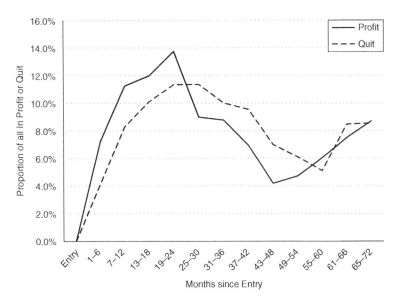

Figure 11.3   *Frequency of outcome by months since entry*[5]

months two in five (40%) report initial profitability. By then over half (55%) have disengaged and the rest, one in 20 (5%), are still active in the start-up process. After six years many still-in-process reach profitability. Others continue to work on their nascent venture, some for more than a decade.

There is, as one might expect, a considerable range in the time to reach profitability or quit, as presented in Figure 11.3. This shows the distribution of the time in process for those nascent ventures that become profitable or disengaged in the first six years.

As can be seen, the largest proportion of both outcomes occurs in the first six months, with two in five (43%) of profitable ventures reaching profitability and one in three (30%) of those that disengage quitting. After the first year, three in five (60%) have reached profitability. Among those that quit, less than half (45%) do so in the first year. These differences are represented in the average values. It takes 14 months to reach profitability but three months longer, 17, to disengage. The major differences, as illustrated in Figure 11.3, is the small proportion of ventures that take more than two years to disengage.

Business creation

Several types of ventures may take longer to reach an outcome. Those that reflect an inexperienced start-up team or one short on resources may require additional time. In addition, a number of efforts are initiated by those that are unsure or ambivalent about an entrepreneurial option. On the other hand, it would not be a surprise if larger and more complicated nascent efforts take longer to reach initial profitability or determine that a venture cannot be profitable. Determining the outcome of a nascent venture is not always quick nor simple.

WHO BECOMES PROFITABLE?

There are some patterns related to the background and situation of the nascent entrepreneur and the outcomes. They can be considered in terms of socio-demographic background, human capital, and financial context.

Perhaps most significant is the lack of any statistical or substantive significance related to gender. As shown in Table 11.2, men and women are almost at parity in achieving initial profitability, although men have a slight advantage, 39% versus 36%.

The relationship to age is more complex. Younger women, under 35 years of age, are more likely to reach profitability than age-peer males. On the other hand, men 35 years and older are more likely to reach profitability than age-peer women. Those least likely to reach profitability are men 18 to 24 years old and men and women over 64 years of age; they are the most likely to have disengaged.

The patterns related to ethnic background is complicated by the small number of Hispanic cases.[6] The proportions that report initial profitability is higher for African-Americans (40%) and Hispanics (48%) than for Whites (37%). Most significant is the low proportion of African-American and Hispanics that have disengaged (38% and 33%). The Mixed, Other category is the least likely to reach profitability (27%) and most likely to quit (63%), but as this is a very diverse group it is difficult to interpret the patterns.

There is virtually no difference related to birth origin: those born in and outside the United States have the same patterns related to outcomes.

Internal migration indicates that those having lived in their county for less than a year are the least likely to reach profitability. Those

Table 11.2   Entrepreneur socio-demographic characteristics and outcomes[7]

	Initial Profitability (%)	Active Start-up (%)	Quit (%)	Statistical Significance (%)
All cases	37.5	13.6	56.8	
Gender				
Men	38.9	14.4	46.7	
Women	35.5	15.4	49.1	ns
Men by Age				
18–24 Years old	25.9	14.0	60.2	
25–34 Years old	30.7	18.8	50.5	
35–44 Years old	53.1	9.7	37.2	
45–54 Years old	29.1	17.7	53.2	
55–64 Years old	48.5	13.6	37.9	
65+ Years old	26.3	10.5	63.2	***
Women by Age				
18–24 Years old	38.5	12.8	48.7	
25–34 Years old	45.4	12.3	42.3	
35–44 Years old	31.9	19.6	48.5	
45–54 Years old	28.9	16.5	54.5	
55–64 Years old	30.3	10.6	59.1	
65+ Years old	12.5	0.0	87.5	*
Ethnic background				
White	37.4	13.1	49.5	
African-American	39.5	23.0	37.5	
Hispanic American	48.0	18.7	33.3	
Mixed/Other	27.3	9.4	63.3	***
U.S. Immigration				
Entrepreneur U.S. born	37.4	15.0	47.7	
Entrepreneur born outside U.S.	39.2	13.5	47.3	ns
County Immigrant, Lived				
Up to 1 year	22.4	23.5	54.1	
2–9 years	43.7	9.9	46.5	
10–29 years	39.0	15.8	45.1	
30+ years	29.9	18.5	51.6	***

Note: Statistical significance: ns = not significant; *=0.05; ***=0.001.

with 30 or more years in their county are slightly more successful, but this measure may be correlated with age: long term residents may be older. Those with 2 to 29 years of residence are the most likely to reach profitability.

The relationship between human capital and outcomes is summarized in Table 11.3. Those with graduate experience are much more likely to reach profitability (46%). While fewer nascent entrepreneurs that have not gone beyond high school reach profitability (33%), this is still an encouraging level of success.

Table 11.3   Entrepreneur human capital and outcomes[8]

	Initial Profitability (%)	Active Start-up (%)	Quit (%)	Statistical Significance
All Cases	37.5	13.6	56.8	
Educational Attainment				
Up to high school degree	33.5	11.9	54.5	
Post-high school, pre-college	38.2	19.7	42.2	
College degree	34.5	11.7	53.8	
Graduate experience	45.9	12.6	41.6	***
Work Status at Entry				
Full-time work for others	32.1	18.9	49.0	
Part-time work for others	41.9	12.8	45.4	
Business owner, self-employed	39.7	12.9	47.5	
Homemaker	31.1	7.6	61.3	
Unemployed	24.6	18.5	56.9	
Student/retired/disabled	28.6	28.6	42.8	***
Same Sector Work Experience				
None	34.4	11.2	54.4	
1–5 years	26.9	13.7	59.4	
6–14 years	41.8	20.6	37.6	
15 or more years	48.9	15.8	35.3	***
Other Start-up Experiences				
None	36.0	12.6	51.4	
One other	35.1	14.9	50.0	
Two or more	44.1	21.3	34.6	***

Note: Statistical significance: ***=0.001.

Two in five (40%) of those with part-time jobs or currently active as business owners or self-employed reach initial profitability. This is higher than any other work status. But better than one in four of those not involved in work—homemakers, the unemployed, and students, retirees or the disabled—reach initial profitability.

Work experience in the same sector as the nascent venture seems to be very helpful. Those with 15 or more years of same sector work experience are the most likely to reach profitability (49%), followed closely (42%) by those with six to 14 years of experience. Those with less than six years of experience appear to be at a disadvantage; two-thirds do not reach profitability.

The major impact of more experience with nascent ventures is that those with two or more other start-ups are more likely to reach profitability (44%), more likely to be active in the start-up process (21%) and only one in three have disengaged. Experience with start-ups seems to have a very positive effect.

There seems to be a positive association between a more secure financial status and reaching profitability, presented in Table 11.4. About a quarter of those nascent entrepreneurs from households with less than $40,000 a year reach profitability, compared to two in five of those from households with higher annual incomes.

The pattern related to household wealth is more nuanced. Over 40% of those with negative or no net worth reach profitability; perhaps they are more motivated to ensure success. Not only are over half of those with the most wealth, $500,000 or more, reaching profitability, but they have a low rate of disengagement. Access to financial resources may facilitate the firm creation process, or these individuals may have other useful attributes, such as higher education or work experience.

WHAT ABOUT THE QUITTERS?

The most likely outcome from participating in business creation is to quit. As shown in Figure 11.2, over half of the nascent ventures have been shut down during the first six years in the start-up process. When asked the primary reason for disengaging from the start-up venture, a wide range of responses were provided, summarized in Table 11.5.

Three of five categories involve issues with the business, which account for 59% of the responses. Two categories are related to the

Table 11.4   Entrepreneur financial context and outcomes[9]

	Initial Profitability (%)	Active Start-up (%)	Quit (%)	Statistical Significance
All Cases	37.5	13.6	56.8	
Household Income (before taxes, $2005)				
Up to $20,000/year	28.4	16.4	55.2	
$20,001 to $40,000/year	26.8	17.4	55.8	
$40,001 to $60,000/year	41.1	12.9	46.0	
$60,001 to $80,000/year	40.1	16.3	43.6	
$80,001 to $100,000/year	47.3	11.2	41.5	
$100,001 to $150,000/year	44.9	9.5	45.6	
$150,001+/year	39.5	18.5	42.0	***
Household Net Worth ($2005)				
Negative, up to $0	42.3	14.1	43.6	
$1 to $25,000	25.8	18.4	55.8	
$25,001 to $100,000	35.3	11.7	53.0	
$100,001 to $200,000	43.9	11.7	44.4	
$200,001 to $500,000	32.2	11.1	56.7	
$500,001 to $1,000,000	56.5	13.7	30.1	
$1,000,001+	51.7	17.2	31.0	***

Note: Statistical significance: ***=0.001.

social context and personal situation of the nascent entrepreneur, which account for 41%.

The major problem related to the business is the lack of customers and income, reported by 32%, which involves attracting interest in the product or service, low revenue, or intense competition. These problems are reported twice as frequently as the next major business category, which is lack of adequate financial support; reported by 15%. This includes a shortfall of initial seed funding or inadequate assistance from financial institutions or investors. The third category of business complications involves the operation of the business itself, reported by 13%. Problems include the loss of a partner or other human resources, inadequate business plan, problems with a location, or, for less than 1%, complications with government regulations.

The major non-business complication, reported by 30%, are a range of personal or family issues, such a health issues or caring for

Table 11.5   Reasons for quitting a start-up venture[10]

	(%)	(%)
Revenue, income shortfall		31.9
Low profits or revenue	11.1	
Low interest or demand for product, service	8.3	
Difficulty marketing, finding, or attracting customers	5.2	
Competition too strong	2.3	
Other product, service sales, and revenue issues	5.0	
Personal and family issues		30.0
Cannot devote required time, demands from other work	9.0	
Personal or family health, caregiving responsibilities	8.2	
Attending or returning to school	4.1	
Lack of interest, lack of motivation	2.8	
Residential relocation	1.0	
Other personal, family issues	4.9	
Financial support		15.4
Insufficient start-up funds	7.7	
Problems acquiring initial financial support	3.3	
Other financial sponsorship issues	4.4	
Organization, administrative, management issues		13.4
Loss of partner, valuable employee, or business contact	4.0	
Complications with or inadequate business plan	1.0	
Government regulations	0.7	
Business location issues, lost or unable to acquire	0.2	
Other organizational, administrative, or management issues	7.5	
Work career options		9.5
Started a new job or new occupation	4.1	
Started a different new business, switched to another start-up	3.0	
Returned to previous job or occupation	0.8	
Other career opportunity related	1.6	
Totals		100.2

a family member, lack of time to devote to the start-up, returning to school or a loss of interest in the project. The second major category is the attraction of other work career options, provided by 10%, which includes getting involved with a different start-up or returning to a job or other occupation. Together these factors, unrelated to the actual start-up venture, account for 45% of those that disengage.

It is to be noted that the two topics that receive the greatest attention in public policy discussions—financial support and regulatory burdens—are not given as major reasons for disengagement. The major challenge is getting customers and generating income. It may be difficult for public policies to have a major impact on the 40% that disengage in response to personal and family issues or other career options.

There are some differences associated with the length of time in the start-up process before disengagement. The pattern presented in Figure 11.4 indicates that those that disengage after four years are

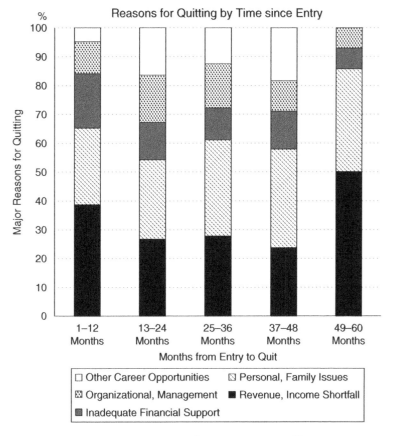

Figure 11.4   Reasons for quitting by time since entry[11]

much more likely to mention income shortfall as a major complication; other career opportunities are mentioned less frequently after four years. Complications involving organizational and management issues are about the same across the six years. Problems with financial support are greatest in the first year and mentioned less frequently in the following three years.

Different reasons for quitting are provided by those with different socio-economic backgrounds, as presented in Table 11.6. For example, there are no real differences between men and women in the mention of personal and family issues, inadequate financial support, or other career options. Women are slightly more likely to mention revenue shortfalls (33% versus 31%) and men are more likely to mention organizational problems (16% versus 10%).

One difference related to age is that those 18 to 24 and 45 to 54 years old are less likely to mention revenue shortfall and more likely to mention family and personal issues. Those 25 to 44 years old are more likely to mention other career options. Those 55 and older give the strongest emphasis to revenue problems.

There are not statistically significant differences related to ethnic categories. Those from all backgrounds report a variety of issues that lead to disengagement.

Those with 15 or more years of same sector work experience are much less likely to mention revenue shortfall as a reason to disengage; they give more emphasis to personal and family issues. There is not much difference associated with years of same sector work experience. Those with less than six years are more likely to report problems with financial support. Those with 15 or more years are more likely to mention personal, or family issues and less likely to mention revenue shortfall.

Those with three or more start-up experiences are less likely to mention revenue short-fall as a major problem. Those on their second start-up are more likely to mention revenue shortfall and family issues, and other problems are mentioned less often.

WHAT DO THEY DO NEXT?

The relationship between socio-demographic characteristics and the post-quit options is presented in Table 11.7. About half (51%) that leave the start-up venture return to their previous job or a new

Table 11.6 Entrepreneur socio-demographic characteristics and reasons for quitting[12]

	Revenue Shortfall (%)	Personal, Family Issues (%)	Inadequate Financial Support (%)	Organizational Problems (%)	Other Career Options (%)	Row Totals (%)	Statistical Significance
All	31.7	30.0	15.3	13.5	9.5	100.0	
Men	30.8	29.4	14.9	15.9	9.0	100.0	
Women	33.0	30.7	15.8	10.2	10.2	99.9	ns
18–24 Years old	23.0	50.8	8.2	11.5	6.6	100.1	
25–34 Years old	39.6	23.1	17.2	6.0	14.2	100.1	
35–44 Years old	34.4	20.6	17.6	13.0	14.5	100.1	
45–54 Years old	18.5	46.3	11.1	21.3	2.8	100.0	
55–64 Years old	43.3	19.4	16.4	19.4	1.5	100.0	***
White	28.9	31.4	14.8	15.7	9.2	100.0	
African-American	44.0	20.0	20.0	6.0	10.0	100.0	
Hispanic	20.0	10.0	40.0	10.0	20.0	100.0	
Mixed, Other	37.3	32.5	12.0	10.8	7.2	99.8	ns
Same sector experience: 0 Years	30.6	21.8	25.0	14.5	8.1	100.0	
Same sector experience: 1–5 Years	34.5	31.4	14.9	9.3	9.8	99.	
Same sector experience: 6–14 Years	36.4	28.3	8.1	14.1	13.1	100.0%	
Same sector experience: 15+ Years	22.4	41.2	9.4	20.0	7.1	100.1	**
First start-up	30.3	24.5	17.3	15.6	12.2	99.9	
Second start-up	39.8	40.6	7.0	8.6	3.9	99.9	
Third or more start-ups	25.6	32.9	20.7	13.4	7.3	99.9	***

Note: Statistical significance: ns = not significant; **=0.01; ***=0.001.

Table 11.7 Entrepreneur socio-demographic characteristics and post-quit options[13]

	Old, New Job (%)	Another Start-up (%)	Leave the Labor Force (%)	Looking for Work (%)	Return to School (%)	Row Totals (%)	Statistical Significance
All	51.4	25.7	17.6	4.0	1.2	99.9	
Men	51.0	28.4	14.9	4.3	1.4	100.0	
Women	52.2	21.7	21.7	3.6	0.7	99.9	ns
18–24 Years old	57.7	7.7	23.1	7.7	3.8	100.0	
25–34 Years old	56.0	20.0	10.7	10.7	2.7	100.1	
35–44 Years old	59.7	31.5	8.1	0.7	0.0	100.1	
45–54 Years old	49.2	15.3	32.2	3.4	0.0	100.1	
55–64 Years old	8.6	45.7	45.7	0.0	0.0	100.0	***
White	54.4	23.4	19.0	3.2	0.0	100.0	
African-American	30.0	43.3	16.7	8.3	1.7	100.0	
Hispanic	85.0	5.0	0.0	0.0	10.0	100.0	
Mixed, Other	53.3	20.0	26.7	0.0	0.0	100.0	***
Same sector experience: 0 Years	54.3	21.7	18.1	4.3	1.4	99.8	
Same sector experience: 1–5 Years	54.5	30.9	9.1	3.6	1.8	99.9	
Same sector experience: 6–14 ears	38.0	48.1	11.4	1.3	1.3	100.1	
Same sector experience: 15+ Years	58.9	5.5	30.1	5.5	0.0	100.0	***
First start-up	65.2	14.0	12.9	6.2	1.7	100.0	
Second start-up	30.5	46.7	21.0	1.9	0.0	100.1	
Third or more start-ups	46.9	25.0	25.0	1.6	1.6	100.1	***

Note: Statistical significance: ns = not significant; ***=0.001.

position. About one in four (24.7%) get involved in another start-up effort. Leaving the labor force to retire or focus on homemaking is reported by about one in six (18%). A small proportion (4%) are looking for work and a few (1%) return to school.

There are few significant differences between men and women. More men get involved in another start-up (28% versus 22%) and women leave the labor force (22% versus 15%).

Returning to school or looking for work is more likely among those under 35 years of age. Those over 54 years old are more likely to pursue another start-up or leave the labor force; none reports looking for work or returning to school.

African-Americans are most likely to pursue another start-up after disengagement. Hispanics, remembering that this is a small sample, are most likely to be employed or return to school.

All those with up to 14 years of work experience have similar post-quit plans, but those with 15 or more years of work experience are more likely to leave the labor force and less likely to pursue another start-up. Those leaving their first start-up are more likely to seek paid work (take a job or look for one) and much less likely to get involved in another start-up. Perhaps it is related to stage in the life course, for those 55 and older, with 15 or more years same sector work experience, or involved in three or more start-ups are most likely to leave the workforce after disengagement.

ARE THEY DISCOURAGED ABOUT START-UPS?

Those that quit are not discouraged. More than a quarter are eager to get involved again and two-thirds say they would try another start-up if the conditions were right. Only one in 12 say never again will they get involved. These responses are summarized in Table 11.8.

This high level of interest in pursuing business creation is present for nascent entrepreneurs from all backgrounds. Men are slightly more likely to want to get involved again, but a larger proportion of women (13% versus 5% for men) never want to be involved in another start-up.

Over one-third of those under 35 years of age are eager for another start-up; almost none says never again. There is reduced interest among those 55 and older: one-fifth never want to be involved in

Table 11.8 Disengaged nascent entrepreneur interest in future start-ups[14]

	Most Certainly (%)	Under Right Conditions (%)	Never Again (%)	Row Total (%)	Statistical Significance
All	25.9	65.7	8.4	100.0	
Men	24.7	70.1	5.2	100.0	
Women	27.6	59.3	13.0	99.9	*
18–24 Years old	33.3	66.7	0.0	100.0	
25–34 Years old	40.0	56.9	3.1	100.0	
35–44 Years old	20.6	65.6	13.7	99.9	
45–54 Years old	23.5	76.5	0.0	100.0	
55–64 Years old	17.9	60.7	21.4	100.0	***
White	24.3	71.2	4.5	100.0	
African-American	27.9	51.2	20.9	100.0	
Hispanic	26.3	68.4	5.3	100.0	
Mixed, Other	50.0	8.3	41.7	100.0	***
Same sector experience: 0 Years	18.5	68.1	13.4	100.0	
Same sector experience: 1–5 Years	32.5	62.5	5.0	100.0	
Same sector experience: 6–14 Years	33.8	63.2	2.9	99.9	
Same sector experience: 15+ Years	26.8	64.8	8.5	100.1	ns
First start-up	21.2	72.7	6.1	100.0	
Second start-up	18.8	74.1	7.1	100.0	
Third or more start-ups	55.3	23.4	21.3	100.0	***

Note: Statistical significance: ns = not significant; *=0.05; ***=0.001.

143

another nascent venture. Almost all those 25 to 54 years old reflect a continuing interest in entrepreneurial options.

While one in four Whites and Hispanics are strongly interested in another start-up; it is higher for African-American and those with a mixed or other background. Those from a mixed or other background reflect a divided response: half want to get involved again but a substantial minority want to avoid nascent ventures in the future. More than half of Whites, African-Americans, and Hispanics would be interested in another start-up under the right conditions.

There is a strong interest among those with varying levels of same sector work experience, although a slightly higher proportion (13% versus 8%) of those with no experience claim "never again." Those that have quit after their first or second start-up are interested in another effort.

Those involved in their first or second start-up are eager to be involved again. Those on their third initiative reflect the greatest diversity: over half are eager for another start-up experience, yet one in five (21%) say they will never again be involved.

One pattern is quite clear, the large majority of those that participated in a start-up that didn't work out would consider another effort, and a substantial proportion are eager to be involved in another start-up.

OVERVIEW

Patterns related to pivoting during the start-up process include:

- A small proportion will adjust their business plan in reaction to new information about their context or operational procedures; those that adjust are more likely to reach profitability.
- Within six years of beginning the start-up process, two in five have reached profitability and slightly more than half have abandoned the initiative. One in 20 are still actively involved.
- Twelve months after beginning the entrepreneurial process, over half that will be profitable are profitable, and almost half of the quits have abandoned the venture. It takes, on average, about three months longer to quit than reach profitability.
- While many from all backgrounds and situations reach

profitability, a number of factors seem to be associated with high potential for success:

- Overall, there is no gender difference, but younger women and older men are more successful.
- Minorities are more likely to reach profitability than the White majority.
- Country of origin has no relationship to profitability.
- Established county residents are more likely to reach profitability.
- Graduate education, part-time work or business management, same sector work experience, and more start-up experience is associated with more profitability.
- Greater household income and net worth is associated with a higher potential for profitability.

● One in five that leave a start-up get involved in another business creation effort. Three in four return to work, either their old job or a new position.

● The majority of those that disengage continue to find the entrepreneurial option attractive. Over nine in ten that leave a start-up would be willing to be involved again. One-fourth would like to pursue another start-up; two-thirds would consider another start-up under the right conditions.

● There is no gender difference related to success in reaching profitability, reasons for disengagement, or interest in future participation.

● There are small differences in experiences related to ethnic background; minorities are generally more successful and committed than the White majority.

Despite the risk that a nascent venture may not become profitable, the entrepreneurial option is very attractive to those that get involved. On the other hand, those pursuing business creation should be prepared to adjust their initial business plan and disengage from the nascent venture. Identifying unprofitable nascent ventures as quickly as possible may be the smartest career strategy.

POLICY IMPLICATIONS

The benefits of business creation reflect the success of the two-fifths of start-up efforts that achieve profitability. It is difficult to predict which efforts will achieve success, suggesting that public policy should:

- Not discourage any reasonable effort.
- Facilitate early identification of efforts that are not viable.
- Minimize the costs of disengagement.
- Support the efforts of disengaged entrepreneurs to participate in another start-up.

Business creation is clearly a core feature of work life in the United States. While less than half of nascent ventures become profitable, it continues to be an attractive option for large segments of the workforce. Given the ongoing contributions to the economy, public policies should continue to support this critical feature of business life.

NOTES

1. At the beginning of each follow-up interview, the first module confirms that the nascent venture has not changed since the last interview. If the nascent entrepreneur reports any change, details about the extent and reason for the adjustment are obtained. As it is more systematic and detailed, only data from PSED II is discussed.
2. Based on PSED II cases' responses to items BA14, CA14, DA14, EA14, FA14, BA17, CA17, DA17, EA17, and FA17. Cases weighted to adjust for screening sampling, start-up team size, and time in process biases (n=29).
3. Based on PSED II cases with information on 72 month outcome status, weight adjusted for screening sampling, start-up team size, and time in process biases (n=760). The difference is not statistically significant.
4. This figure is based on the two U.S. data sets (1999,2005) in Reynolds, et al., (2016), number of cases with data varies from 1,418 (entry) to 1,241 (72 months). For computing the outcome proportions for each time period, cases without data are excluded. Weights represent the nascent ventures with outcome data adjusted to correct for screening sampling, team size, and time in process biases.
5. See endnote 4 to Figure 11.2.
6. Data is available on 765 White, 177 African-Americans, 59 Hispanic, and 122 Mixed, Other respondents.
7. All characteristics harmonized across both U.S. PSED I and II data sets. Only cases with data on outcomes are included (n=1,418). Case weights represent nascent entrepreneurs and were adjusted for biases in sample screening and duration in the start-up process.

8. All characteristics harmonized across both U.S. PSED I and II data sets. Only cases with data on outcomes are included (n varied from 1,324 to 1,418). Case weights represent nascent entrepreneurs and were adjusted for biases in sample screening and duration in the start-up process. Respondents were allowed to select multiple labor force relationships, that is, they could be both disabled and a homemaker. A single labor force participation was selected for each case in the order of full-time work, part-time work, business owner or self-employed, homemaker, unemployed, and student/retired/disabled.
9. All values are in 2005 U.S. dollars; 1999 values adjusted using the consumer price index. Case weights representing nascent entrepreneurs were adjusted to compensate for biases in sample screening and duration in the start-up process. Household income assessment based on 1,319 cases and household net worth assessment based on 1,170 cases.
10. Data based on U.S. PSED II data open ended items (BE52, CE52, DE52, EE52, and FE52) coded by the University of Michigan Institute for Survey Research staff and available at www.psed.isr.umich.edu. Weights adjusted for screening sample, start-up team size, and time in process biases (n= 504).
11. See Table 11.5 and endnote 10. Cases adjusted for screening sampling and time in process biases (n=452).
12. See Table 11.5 and endnote 10. Based on PSED II responses. Cases adjusted for screening sampling and time in process bias (n=504).
13. Data based on U.S. PSED I data fixed response items on the website at www.psed.isr.umich.edu (R545, S545, and T545), adjusted for screening sampling and time in process biases (n=346).
14. Based on responses to R546, S546, and T546 by PSED I respondents, adjusted for screening sampling, start-up team size, and time in process biases (n=297).

12. Overview

Committed nascent entrepreneurs, those serious about seeing if they can create a new business, are the majority of those pursuing business creation. Exploratory nascent entrepreneurs, who are making tentative steps but are not sure about this career choice, are a substantial minority. In either case, there are ten things to know about the entrepreneurial experience.

1. *It can be very satisfying.* The sense of satisfaction and self-confidence among those that create successful businesses is obvious at every turn. Further, most that get involved and discover that their initiatives may not be viable find it a rewarding experience and often pursue other start-up efforts. On the other hand, it is not for everybody and in most developed countries the majority do not participate in business creation.
2. *Everybody gets involved; some more than others.* There is no age, gender, or ethnic group that is not represented among business creators. While most nascent entrepreneurs are men from 25 to 40 years old, a substantial proportion are women. Further, every age group including young adults, established adults, and even retirees become involved. Both ethnic minorities and immigrants are very active, although the established majorities are the largest proportion of active nascent entrepreneurs. Participation is much more likely among those that see business opportunities, know others involved in business creation, and are confident of their entrepreneurial skills.
3. *Motives are diverse and may change.* Most people that become involved are responding to the economic context: some seek promising business opportunities while others consider their existing work options as unsatisfactory. There is often a mixture of personal or intrinsic motives, including a desire for independence, interest in implementing a new idea, a preference for wealth, or a desire to gain respect. As they move through the

start-up process, individuals' motives may change. While few entrepreneurs are attracted to risk, many are willing to accept some risk for a significant payoff.

4. *It is a social experience*. Despite the media image of the entrepreneur as a lone economic gunslinger taking on the competition, the most successful efforts involve start-up teams and a supportive social network. While start-up teams of business partners tend to be more successful than teams of family members, both may be more successful than the lone operator. But all start-up efforts benefit from a supporting social network of suppliers and mentors.

5. *Know what you are doing*. The single most important personal factor associated with creating a profitable start-up is business experience, preferably in the industry in which the start-up will compete. The vast majority of new businesses will compete in established industries, and each sector has a range of distinctive, critical features required for success. The more industry experience among the start-up team, the greater the potential for profitability. The rare exceptions are situations where the new firm is creating a new market or industry segment and there is no competition. While some of these "industry creating" start-ups have dramatic success, for example Facebook, these are rare.

6. *Do it!* Starting a business involves a decision not to pursue other options, either a job or another start-up venture. These foregone opportunities are a major opportunity cost for the start-up team. The fastest way to determine whether the new venture will be successful is to take action to implement the business. The sooner a variety of relevant start-up activities are implemented, the sooner the outcome can be determined and the lower the opportunity cost.

7. *Some activities are more helpful than others*. Creating a new firm involves implementing a wide range of start-up activities. Those that involve developing a public presence for the new venture, identifying the reaction of customers, and creating the business infrastructure for providing the goods or services seem to facilitate attaining initial profitability. Business planning and seeking external funding are useful, particularly in identifying nascent ventures that may not be profitable, but are less critical in reaching profitability.

8. *It takes some effort.* New firms are seldom created overnight. It generally takes some effort. The typical start-up that achieves profitability takes about nine person-months of effort and $26,000, shared among the start-up team. Complicated efforts may require more resources and more time for technical development. As a result, it may take several years to achieve initial profitability; six years after initiating a new start-up one-in-twenty have not reached a clear outcome.

9. *Money may be necessary, but is not sufficient.* Four in five start-ups receive informal funding, but less than half become registered as legal entities that can receive formal funding. Less than half of registered ventures, or less than one-fifth of the total, receive formal financial support the year after they are legal entities. While the total of informal and formal financial support averages $68,000 in equity and $106,000 in debt, there is substantial variation.[1] A small fraction raise millions. While more than seven in ten nascent ventures with over $25,000 in formal funding reach profitability, three in five of profitable new ventures have no formal funding.[2]

10. *Profits are elusive, prepare to pivot.* About two in five nascent ventures reach profitability. Adjustment of the business idea, or pivoting during the start-up process, may do much to facilitate success. Three in five that discontinue do so for business complications; the major challenges of attracting paying customers, inadequate financial support or organizational problems are each reported by one in six. Two in five disengage in response to personal or family issues, reported by three in ten, or the attraction of other career options. Most nascent entrepreneurs that quit, however, are willing or eager to get involved in another nascent venture.

COMMENTARY

Most involved in an entrepreneurial experience find it very satisfying. For many starting out, a new business is exciting and profitable. Others gain knowledge and proficiency. Patterns found among those engaged in business creation suggest strategies that can minimize the costs associated with these life changing transitions.

POLICY IMPLICATIONS

The major policy goals are usually to gain the benefits of business creation, including economic adaptation and innovation, job growth, improved productivity, and more satisfied people in the workforce. There are several features of the process that may be addressed. First, how to get more people to pursue entrepreneurial careers and commit to new firm creation. Second, how to facilitate the transition from a start-up initiative to a profitable new firm. Third, how to reduce the social costs associated with business creation.

Get More Start-ups

People start businesses. The more people that become involved, the more businesses. While business creation is currently a very popular career option in the United States, a number of activities may increase participation.

- Recognize the contributions of responsible business creation.
- Promote satisfaction of those making this career choice.
- No social category should be discouraged.
- Formal training in educational programs legitimates entrepreneurship as socially valued.
- Encourage all to get involved, regardless of variation in personality or stated motivations, risk preference, or cognitive orientations.
- Minimize costs of disengagement.
- Facilitate additional career options if a nascent venture doesn't work out.

Facilitate Profitable Outcomes

Once a start-up team begins the business creation process, they can reduce the sunk cost in time and money by:

- Acquiring training in business creation and management.
- Creating a social network, either of team members or supportive others, to broaden the knowledge base and social contacts that can facilitate the start-up process.

- Testing the business idea with future customers as quickly as possible.
- Moving as quickly as possible on all major start-up requirements.
- Pursuing legal registration early in the process to facilitate formal financial support.

Minimize the Social Costs of Business Creation

The majority of sweat equity (time on task) and informal financial support devoted to firm creation is invested in nascent ventures that never make it. This is a sunk cost that can never be recovered. This social cost can be minimized in several ways.

- Facilitate creating a profitable new firm, as suggested above.
- Encourage nascent venture teams to adjust their business plan as they receive additional information.
- Emphasize moving forward with the business creation process quickly and on multiple dimensions to determine viability at the earliest possible moment.
- Be realistic about the firm's potential and disengage as soon as negative feedback is substantial, such as an inability to attract customers or obtain formal financing.

NOTES

1. See Table 10.2.
2. See Figure 10.4.

Appendix: U.S. PSED data sets

An empirically based analysis of the business creation process requires at least two elements: it must be based on representative samples of all potential start-ups, both those that succeed and those that ultimately quit, and it must observe the startup process over time to determine how and why some achieve profitability and others do not.

The PSED protocol involved, after extensive field testing, several procedures. First, those active in the pre-profit stage of business creation are located with a screening module completed by representative samples of adults. Not only does this provide confidence that the sample represents business creation in the population, it also facilitates extrapolation from the sample to the total population. This allows for estimates of the total number of individuals or resources involved. Those active in business creation complete a detailed interview shortly after being identified in the screening.

The second feature is the follow-up interviews, usually every 12 months, to determine the outcome of the effort to implement a new business. This provides evidence of the success of these efforts. Those that report profitable new firms provide details about their contributions to job creation, exports, and value added.

Extensive data sets were developed in two large scale panels in the United States, U.S. PSED I in 1999 and U.S. PSED II in 2005.[1] A summary of the screening and follow-up interview case counts is presented in Table A.1.[2] To minimize costs, those respondents that indicated they had disengaged from a start-up effort in a follow-up interview were not contacted in subsequent interviews.

Several complications require attention to provide a useful analysis. First, not all individuals located in the population screening qualify as active nascent entrepreneurs. Some individuals report very low levels of activity, management of a venture that had already reached profitability, or beginning the business creation process ten years prior to the screening interview. These cases are set aside to ensure a more homogeneous cohort.

Table A.1 *PSED cohort development overview*

	PSED I	PSED II	Total
Screening Initiated	Jul 1998	Oct 2005	
Screening Completed	Jan 2000	Jan 2006	
Comparison group: Adult population	223		
Comparison group: Minority only	208		
Nascent screening sample	62,612	31,845	94,457
Screening identified nascents	a1,492	1,587	3,079
Completed Wave 1 interview	830	1,214	2,044
Completed Wave 2 interview	501	972	1,473
Completed Wave 3 interview	511	746	1,257
Completed Wave 4 interview	533	527	1,060
Completed Wave 5 interview		435	435
Completed Wave 6 interview		375	375
One or more follow-up interviews	695	1,110	1,805
One or more follow-up interviews, %	83.7	91.4	88.3
Wave 1 to Wave 2 lag: Months (average)	13.1	12.4	
Wave 1 to Wave 3 lag: Months (average)	29.3	25.2	
Wave 1 to Wave 4 lag: Months (average)	53.4	37.4	
Wave 1 to Wave 5 lag: Months (average)		49.6	
Wave 1 to Wave 6 lag: Months (average)		61.3	

Note: a. U.S. PSED I had three screening procedures. The first selected all eligible nascent entrepreneurs, the second only female nascent entrepreneurs, and the third only Black or Hispanic nascent entrepreneurs. As a result, a large number of those identified as nascent entrepreneurs were not included in the cohort. Case weights provide an adjustment to match the gender and ethnic proportions in the adult population.

Second, because nascent entrepreneurs are at different stages of the start-up process when they are identified in the screening interview, the multi-wave data collection covers an arbitrary portion of the business creation window. This window of observation differs for every case in the data file. In order to harmonize the start-up window across all cases, each case is assigned a conception date. This date of entry into the start-up process is case specific and independent of the date when the interviews were completed.

Third, a small proportion of cases that complete the first detailed

Table A.2   Cohorts reorganized by business creation time line

	U.S. PSED I	U.S. PSED II	Total
Screening Initiated	Jul 1998	Oct 2005	
Screening Completed	Jan 2000	Jan 2006	
Nascent screening sample	62,612	31,845	94,457
Screening identified nascents	1,492	1,587	3,079
Completed Wave 1 interview	830	1,214	2,044
One or more follow-up interviews	695	1,110	1,805
Active nascent entrepreneurs	665	902	1,567
1 Month: Active nascents & follow-up	569	860	1,429
12 Month: Active nascents & follow-up	565	856	1,421
24 Month: Active nascents & follow-up	549	845	1,394
36 Month: Active nascents & follow-up	541	818	1,359
48 Month: Active nascents & follow-up	524	801	1,325
60 Month: Active nascents & follow-up	496	782	1,278
72 Month: Active nascents & follow-up	419	712	1,131

interview, about 12%, could not be contacted for any follow-up interview. The data set is, therefore, restricted to the 88% of the cases for which data is available from at least one follow-up interview. There was a total of 1,567 cases of active nascent entrepreneurs for which follow-up data was available.

The structure of the revised data set, reflecting these adjustments, is presented in Table A.2, which indicates the case counts from entry into the start-up process for the following 72 months.

IDENTIFYING DATE OF ENTRY

The implementation and timing of 19 start-up activities was harmonized across the PSED I and PSED II cohorts.[3] Eighteen activities, excluding initial serious thought about starting a business, were used to identify the earlier of two activities that occurred within a 12 month period. This was considered the date of entry into the process. This date was, on average, 17 months before the initial detailed interview. The transition to a new firm was dated as the first of three (PSED I) or six (PSED II) months when monthly revenue covered all expenses and financially supported the owners. Date of disengagement was based on the respondents' reports of no further work on the start-up. Those ventures that did not report initial profitability or disengagement were considered to be still active in the start-up process; the date of the last follow-up interview was used as the last date the venture was active in the start-up process.

CASE WEIGHTS

There were several stages to the development of case weights.

Case Weights: Sample Screening Adjustment

First, adjustments to compensate for bias in the initial screening. Screening sample case weights were developed so the sample would reflect the major characteristics of the adult population. These weights were then carried over to the cohort of nascent entrepreneurs.

Case Weights: Team Size Adjustment

Second, as those start-ups to be implemented by a larger team were more likely to be represented in a screening to locate team members, the population case weights were adjusted to reduce the impact of those nascent ventures being implemented by larger start-up teams.[4] In most assessments, this adjustment has a small effect on descriptions or analysis.

Case Weights: Duration in Process Adjustment

A third adjustment compensates for the fact that the initial screening identifies nascent entrepreneurs at an arbitrary point in the start-up process. Some will manage to reach an outcome in several months, others may take several years. Those that take longer to implement a new firm are more likely to be included in the initial screening. If those that take longer are less prepared and short on resources, or are working on more complicated ventures, it could affect inferences based on the cohort.

Adjustment for this involves identifying the length of time between entry into the process and the outcome, either initial profitability or discontinuation.[5] For those cases with at least one follow-up interview without an outcome, considered still active in the start-up process, the end date is considered the last interview. Total cases before eliminating those that may not qualify as current active nascent entrepreneurs is 1,647.

Identifying the date of entry involved assessing the start-up activity for each venture. The result was a small number of cases (24) where the outcome data was before the date of entry or (three cases) with durations of less than one month. Duration for these 27 cases (1.6%) was set to one month. There were 72 cases (4.4%) with durations greater than 120 months (ten years). Seventy percent of these cases were those still start-up active, about 15% had reached profitability, and 15% were abandoned. To minimize the effect of very long cases, extreme values are reset to 120 months (ten years).

The weights adjusted to compensate for biases in the screening process and variations in start-up team size were then divided by the months in the start-up process. Those cases longer in the start-up process would then have less impact compared to those cases that reached an outcome quickly.

Finally, the weights were re-centered so the average value was one; the sum of the weights would then equal the sum of the cases. This ensures that the inferences about statistical significance, and analysis procedures that utilize such criteria, are not biased.

Impact of Duration in Process Weights Adjustment

The adjustment for duration in the start-up process had a major impact on any assessment related to the outcome for the nascent ventures. The impact of four cases weight alternates is presented in Table A.3. The comparison is restricted to only those cases with the triple adjusted weights, for sampling, start-up team size, and duration in the start-up process. The slight variation in case counts reflects rounding errors associated with some large weights.

It is clear from Table A.3 that adjustments for potential bias in the screening sample or the greater likelihood that nascent ventures with larger start-up teams may be incorporated into the sample have modest effects on the proportion of cases with different outcomes.

*Table A.3   Effect of alternate case weights on start-up process
            outcomes*

Outcome	No Weights	Screening Adjusted Weights	Screening, Team Size Adjusted Weights	Screening, Team Size, and Duration in Project Adjusted Weights[6]
No cases	1,418	1,420	1,420	1,418
Profitability	24.0%	24.4%	22.9%	35.7%
Start-up Active	35.8%	33.8%	34.3%	15.8%
Quit	40.3%	41.8%	42.8%	48.4%
	100.1%	100.0%	100.0%	99.9%

The adjustment reflecting different durations in the start-up process, however, has a major impact, increasing the proportion that reach profitability from less than one-fourth (24%) to more than one-third (36%). The other major shift is the reduction in proportion identified as active in the start-up process, reduced from one-third (34%) to one-sixth (16%).

This is reflected in the dramatic shifts of estimated time in the start-up process, illustrated in Table A.4. This presents the average time in process for the sample with no weights and three different weighting schemes. Again, only cases with the triple adjusted weights are included. While there are some small differences between the average times to outcome between the first three columns, they are quite similar, indicating that the average time to profitability is about 30 months, the average time to quit about 33 months, and the average time for those active in the process at about 68 months.

There is, however, a substantial change in the far right column, which represents case weights adjusted for time in the start-up process. In this case, the average time to reach profitability is 14 months, the average time to disengage is 18 months, and the average time active in the start-up process is 47 months. These are all substantial reductions from estimates based on no weights or the other two weighting schemes.

The major impact of the triple-adjusted case weights is to reduce

Table A.4   *Effect of alternate case weights on time in the start-up process*

Outcome	No Weights (Average months)	Screening Adjusted Weights (Average months)	Screening, Team Size Adjusted Weights (Average months)	Screening, Team Size, and Duration in Project Adjusted Weights (Average months)
No cases	1,418	1,420	1,420	1,418
Profitability	30.7	30.3	30.5	13.8
Start-up Active	69.5	67.7	67.9	47.4
Quit	33.5	33.4	33.4	18.1
All outcomes	45.7	44.2	44.6	21.2

the impact of those cases that remain in the start-up process and do not reach either initial profitability or disengage.

Sources of Time in Duration Variation

Two sets of factors affecting duration in the process are considered: those related to the venture and those related to the nascent entrepreneurs involved.

The relationship between seven characteristics of the nascent venture and duration in the start-up process is presented in Table A.5. All cases with outcome data are included, and each case is given an equal weight. Nascent ventures with follow-up data are sorted into three process duration categories: up to 2 years, 3 to 5 years, and over 5 years. The first column presents the proportion of nascent ventures in each category for each characteristic.

The growth aspirations has a statistically significant relationship to time in the process; those ventures established to maximize growth appear to spend more time in the start-up process. While not statistically significant, four other factors have suggestive effects. Compared to one person efforts, those with two or more team members may spend less time in the process. Family and collegial teams may be quicker than sole proprietors or spousal pairs. Start-up ventures with no technological focus may be quicker to reach an

Table A.5   *Nascent venture factors associated with duration in*
          process

	Cases (%)	0–2 Years	3–5 Years	Over 5 years	Row Totals (%)	Statistical Significance
Number of Cases (total =1,647)		588	552	507		
		35.7%	33.5%	30.8%	100.0	
Team size						
One human	51.7	34.5%	34.2%	31.3%	100.0	
Two humans	36.2	37.2%	32.3%	30.5%	100.0	
Three humans	6.1	37.0%	36.0%	27.0%	100.0	
Four humans	4.3	33.8%	28.2%	38.0%	100.0	
Five or more humans	1.7	39.3%	42.9%	17.9%	100.1	ns
	100.0					
Team Structure						
Sole proprietorship	51.8	34.3%	34.3%	31.3%	99.9	
Spousal pair	23.6	33.9%	32.4%	33.7%	100.0	
Family team	7.8	39.1%	37.5%	23.4%	100.0	
Collegial team	16.8	40.8%	30.7%	28.5%	100.0	ns
	100.0					
Growth Aspirations						
Keep size easy to manage	79.6	37.4%	32.8%	29.8%	100.0	
Maximize growth	20.4	30.1%	36.1%	33.7%	99.9	*
	100.0					
Technological Emphasis						
None	48.3	37.6%	34.2%	28.2%	100.0	
Low	30.1	33.9%	32.1%	33.9%	99.9	
Some	16.6	34.1%	33.0%	33.0%	100.1	
Highest	5.1	33.3%	36.9%	29.8%	100.0	ns
	100.1					
Economic Sector						
Extractive	4.0	24.6%	36.9%	38.5%	100.0	
Transformation	20.1	40.7%	30.4%	28.9%	100.0	
Business services	31.4	35.9%	32.7%	31.4%	100.0	
Consumer services	44.6	34.4%	35.1%	30.5%	100.0	ns
	100.1					

Table A.5   (continued)

	Cases (%)	0–2 Years	3–5 Years	Over 5 years	Row Totals (%)	Statistical Signific-ance
Team Hours before Outcome						
None	37.2	12.4%	33.3%	54.3%	100.0	
1–500 hours	25.5	42.4%	31.9%	25.7%	100.0	
501–4,000 hours	27.4	27.7%	41.3%	31.0%	100.0	
4,001+ hours	9.9	14.3%	33.9%	51.8%	100.0	***
	100.0					
Team Funding before Outcome						
None to $1,000	26.3	59.1%	29.2%	11.7%	100.0	
$1,001 to $15,000	44.5	37.0%	41.2%	21.8%	100.0	
$15,001 to maximum	29.1	39.2%	36.0%	24.9%	100.1	***
	99.9					

Note: All case weights = 1. Statistical significance: ns = none; * = 0.05; *** = 0.001.

outcome. The small proportion (4%) in extractive sectors appear to take longer, particularly when compared to those in transformative sectors (construction, manufacturing, transportation, wholesale).

Two indicators of the scope and complexity of the business venture are in the bottom two sets of rows in Table A.5. These two measures are total hours invested by the start-up team before the outcome is determined from the PSED I data set and the total funds invested by the start-up team before the outcome is determined from the PSED II data set.[7] Both have a statistically significant relationship to time in process.

But ventures long in the process appear to be of two types. First are those that receive very little start-up team investments. Over half (54%) of those ventures receiving no time commitment from the start-up team have a start-up duration of five or more years. These are the ventures that have a long period of being an "active start-up."

The second type are those that receive a substantial commitment. Over half (51%) of those associated with over 4,000 hours of work are in the start-up process for five or more years. One-quarter (25%) of those nascent ventures that receive more than $15,000 in start-up team financial support are in process for five or more years; longer than any ventures receiving less of an investment.

In contrast, those nascent ventures that are in process for shorter periods of time, up to two years, tend to receive up to 500 hours of attention and less than $15,000 from the start-up team.

A similar assessment related to six characteristics of the start-up team is provided in Table A.6. Four of the six features have a statistically significant relationship.

The strongest relationship is associated with the start-up teams, past experiences with business creation. Those teams with experiences with four or more other start-ups take somewhat longer in the process. A similar pattern, also statistically significant, is related to past same industry work experience. Those teams with more work experience take longer in the process. These two measures may reflect work on more complex, elaborate ventures, which may take longer to implement. Further, the proportion of ventures with these characteristics, 25% and 13%, is large enough to have an impact on the average values.

Two other factors are statistically significant. Teams composed of both young adults and established adults appear to move through the process more quickly; those consisting of individuals 35 and older seem to take a little longer. Compared to White only and White and Minority start-up teams, Minority only start-up teams are in the start-up process a little longer. There is no substantive or statistically significant difference related to working full-time while pursuing a start-up or the gender of the start-up team.

Overall, the only factors with a significant relationship to time in the start-up process are indicators of start-up team investment. Ventures long in the start-up process are either receiving little attention from the start-up team or higher levels of time and financial investments. The use of case weights adjusted to correct for potential bias related to time in the process provides more accurate descriptions of the population of nascent ventures.

ACCESS TO PSED I AND II DATA SETS AND DOCUMENTATION

Full details on all PSED I and II interview schedules, including the phone screening interview, initial and follow-up phone interviews, and mail questionnaires utilized in PSED I, as well as the codebooks and complete data sets (in SPSS, SYSTAT, and SAS formats) are available at no cost on the project website (www.psed.isr.umich.edu).

Table A.6 Start-up team factors associated with duration in process

	Cases (%)	0–2 Years	3–5 Years	Over 5 Years	Row Totals (%)	Statistical Significance
Number of Cases (total = 1,647)		588	552	507		
		35.7%	33.5%	30.8%	100.0	
Working, Managing Full-Time						
Yes	72.9	35.0%	33.8%	31.2%	100.0	
No	27.1	37.7%	32.7%	29.6%	100.0	ns
	100.0					
Gender Composition						
Male only	40.4	36.5%	35.5%	28.0%	100.0	
Mixed	32.7	35.1%	32.0%	32.9%	100.0	
Female Only	27.0	35.1%	32.4%	32.4%	99.9	ns
	100.1					
Team Age Composition						
Only 18–34 years old	22.3	37.5%	36.4%	26.0%	99.9	
Both 18–34 and 35 and older	12.1	42.1%	32.0%	25.9%	100.0	
Only 35 and older	65.6	34.0%	32.5%	33.6%	100.1	*
	100.0					
Team Ethnic Composition						
White only	70.4	37.7%	31.6%	30.7%	100.0	
White and minority	6.6	38.0%	36.1%	25.9%	100.0	
Minority only	23.1	28.9%	38.7%	32.4%	100.0	*
	100.1					
Team Start-up Experiences						
None	37.5	37.0%	34.5%	28.5%	100.0	
1–3 other start-ups	37.4	38.6%	34.9%	26.5%	100.0	
4 or more other start-ups	25.1	29.5%	30.0%	40.6%	100.1	***
	100.0					
Team Start-up Industry Experience						
Up to 5 years	40.9	38.7%	35.0%	26.3%	100.0	
6–30 years	46.3	33.6%	32.4%	34.1%	100.1	
Over 30 years	12.8	33.8%	32.9%	33.3%	100.0	*
	100.0					

Note: All case weights = 1. Statistical significance: ns = none; * = 0.05; *** = 0.001.

NOTES

1. Background on the PSED I initiative is documented in Gartner, Shaver, Carter, and Reynolds (2004) and an overview of the PSED II project is provided in Reynolds and Curtin (2009b).
2. Data on timing, comparison groups, and total screening samples are based on respective chapters in Reynolds and Curtin (2009b, 2010) and Reynolds et al. (2016).
3. This was part of a project that harmonized data across five PSED cohorts from four countries (Reynolds et al., 2016).
4. Discussed in more detail in Ruef (2010), Appendix B.
5. This procedure was a modification of that first described by Shim and Davidsson (2018).
6. The outcome proportions in Table A.3 reflects all cases regardless of time in process. These are different from the proportions presented in Table 11.2, which omit cases without outcome data for each time period.
7. Total start-up team hours before outcome is based only on PSED I cases (n=565), and total start-up team financial commitments before outcome based only on PSED II cases (n=649).

References

Blanchflower, David G. and Andrew J. Oswald. (1998). What Makes an Entrepreneur? *Journal of Labor Economics* 16(1):26–60.

Evans, David S. and Linda S. Leighton. (1989). Some Empirical Aspects of Entrepreneurship. *American Economic Review* 79(3):5 19–535.

Frese, Michael and Michael M. Gielnik. (2014). The Psychology of Entrepreneurship. *Annual Review of Organizational Psychology and Organizational Behavior* 1:413–438.

Gartner, W. B. (1989). "Who is an Entrepreneur?" is the Wrong Question. *Entrepreneurial Theory and Practice* 13(4):47–68.

Gartner, W. B., K. G. Shaver, N. M. Carter, and P. D. Reynolds (Eds). (2004). *Handbook of Entrepreneurial Dynamics: The Process of Business Creation*. Thousand Oaks, CA: Sage Publications.

Global Entrepreneurship Research Association. (2017). Global Entrepreneurship Monitor: 2016/2017 Global Report, accessed June 2, 2018 at www.gemconsortium.org.

Granovetter, Mark. (1955). *Getting a Job: A Study of Contacts and Careers*. Chicago, IL: University of Chicago Press.

Hegedus, Chris and Jehane Noujaim. (2001). *Stareup.com: A film.* Santa Monica, CA: Artisan Home Entertainment.

Johnson, Kevin L., Wade M. Danis, and Marc J. Dollinger. (2004). Decision-making (Innovator/Adaptor) Style. Chapter 13 in Gartner, W. B., K. G. Shaver, N. M. Carter, and P. D. Reynolds (Eds). *Handbook of Entrepreneurial Dynamics: The Process of Business Creation*. Thousand Oaks, CA: Sage Publications, pp. 171–178.

Johnson, Kevin L., Marne L. Arthaud-Day, Joseph C. Rode, and Janet Near. (2004). Job and Life Satisfaction. Chapter 14 in Gartner, W. B., K. G. Shaver, N. M. Carter, and P. D. Reynolds (Eds). *Handbook of Entrepreneurial Dynamics: The Process of Business Creation.* Thousand Oaks, CA: Sage Publications, pp. 163–170.

Kelley, Donna, Slavica Singer, and Mike Herrington. (2016). Global Entrepreneurship Monitor: 2015/2016 Global Report. Global

Entrepreneurship Research Association, accessed June 2, 2018 at www.gemconsortium.org.

Lange, Thomas. (2012). Job Satisfaction and Self-employment: Autonomy or Personality? *Small Business Economics* 38:165–177.

Liao, Jainwen and Harold Welsch. (2004). Entrepreneurial Intensity. Chapter 17 in Gartner, W. B., K. G. Shaver, N. M. Carter, and P. D. Reynolds (Eds). *Handbook of Entrepreneurial Dynamics: The Process of Business Creation.* Thousand Oaks, CA: Sage Publications, pp. 186–195.

McClelland, D. C. (1961). *The Achieving Society*. New York: The Free Press.

Morgan, James N. (2004). On Economic Sophistication. Chapter 20 in Gartner, W. B., K. G. Shaver, N. M. Carter, and P. D. Reynolds (Eds). *Handbook of Entrepreneurial Dynamics: The Process of Business Creation.* Thousand Oaks, CA: Sage Publications, pp. 214–219.

National Science Foundation. (2016). NSF Innovation Corps, accessed June 2, 2018 at www.nsf.gov/news/.

National Technical Information Service. (2002). North American Industry Classification System: United States. Springfield, VA: National Technical Information Service.

Osterwalder, Alexander and Yves Pigneur. (2013). *Business Model Generation: A Handbook for Visionaries, Game Changers, and Challengers.* New York: Wiley.

Polgreen, Lydia. (2011). Scaling Caste Walls with Capitalism's Ladders in India. *International New York Times*, 21 December.

Reiss, Eric. (2011). *The Lean Start-up.* New York City: Penguin Random House, Crown Business.

Reynolds, Paul D. (2007). *Entrepreneurship in the US: The Future is Now.* New York: Springer.

Reynolds, Paul D. (2011a). Informal and Early Formal Financial Support in the Business Creation Process: Exploration with the PSED II Data Set. *Journal of Small Business Management* 49(1):27–54.

Reynolds, Paul D. (2011b). New Firm Creation: A Global Assessment of National, Contextual, and Individual Factors. *Foundations and Trends in Entrepreneurship* 6(5–6):315–496.

Reynolds, Paul D. (2012a). Entrepreneurship in Developing Economies: The Bottom Billions and Business Creation. *Foundations and Trends in Entrepreneurship* 8(3): 141–277.

Reynolds, Paul D. (2012b). Firm Creation in the Business Life Course: MENA Countries in the Global Context. Report submitted to International Development Research Center (Ottawa, Canada) and Organisation for Economic Co-operation and Development (Paris: France).

Reynolds, Paul D. (2015). Business Creation Stability: Why is it so Hard to Increase Entrepreneurship? *Foundations and Trends in Entrepreneurship* 10(5–6):321–475.

Reynolds, Paul D. (2016). Start-up Actions and Outcomes: What Entrepreneurs Do to Reach Profitability. *Foundations and Trends in Entrepreneurship* 12(6):443–559.

Reynolds, Paul D. (2017). When is a Firm Born? Alternative Criteria and Consequences. *Business Economics* 52(1):41–56. DOI: 10.1057/s11369-017-0022-8.

Reynolds, Paul D. and Richard T. Curtin. (2008). Business Creation in the United States: Panel Study of Entrepreneurial Dynamics II Initial Assessment, *Foundations and Trends in Entrepreneurship*. 4(3):155–307.

Reynolds, Paul D. and Richard T. Curtin. (2009a). Business Creation in the United States: Entry, Startup Activities, and the Launch of New Ventures. Chapter 7 in *U.S. Small Business Administration, the Small Business Economy: A Report to the President 2008*. Washington, DC: U.S. Government Printing Office, pp. 165–240.

Reynolds, Paul D. and Richard T. Curtin. (Eds) (2009b). *New Firm Creation in the U.S.: Initial Explorations with the PSED II Data Set.* New York: Springer.

Reynolds, Paul D. and Richard T. Curtin (Eds) (2010). *New Firm Creation: An International Overview*. New York: Springer.

Reynolds, Paul D. and Diana Hechavarria. (2016). Global Entrepreneurship Monitor [GEM]: Adult Population Survey Data Set, 1998-2012. ICPSR20320-v4. Ann Arbor, MI: Inter-university Consortium for Political and Social Research, 2016-12-14, accessed May 15, 2018 at http://doi.org/10.3886/ICPSR20320.v4.

Reynolds, Paul D., Diana Hechavarria, Li Tian, Mikael Samuelsson, and Per Davidsson. (2016) Panel Study of Entrepreneurial Dynamics: A five Cohort Outcomes Harmonized Data Set. Research Gate: DOI: 10.13140/RG.2.1.2561.7682.

Reynolds, Paul D., Sammis B. White, and others. (1993). Wisconsin's Entrepreneurial Climate Study: Final Report. Milwaukee, WI:

Center for the Study of Entrepreneurship, Marquette University. Research Gate: DOI: 10.13140/RG.2.2.10149.09444.

Rose, David S. (2014). *Angel Investing: The Gust Guide to Making Money and Having Fun Investing in Startups.* New York: Wiley.

Ruef, Martin. (2010). *The Entrepreneurial Group: Social Identities, Relations, and Collective Action.* Princeton, NJ: Princeton University Press.

Schumpeter, J. A. (1934). *The Theory of Economic Development.* Cambridge, MA: Harvard University Press.

Shaver, Kelly G. (2004a). Attribution and Locus of Control. Chapter 19 in Gartner, W. B., K. G. Shaver, N. M. Carter, and P. D. Reynolds (Eds). *Handbook of Entrepreneurial Dynamics: The Process of Business Creation.* Thousand Oaks, CA: Sage Publications, pp. 205–213.

Shaver, Kelly G. (2004b). Overview: The Cognitive Characteristics of the Entrepreneur. Chapter 11 in Gartner, W. B., K. G. Shaver, N. M. Carter, and P. D. Reynolds (Eds). *Handbook of Entrepreneurial Dynamics: The Process of Business Creation.* Thousand Oaks, CA: Sage Publications, pp. 131–141.

Shim, Jaehu and Per Davidsson. (2018). Shorter Than We Thought: The Duration of Venture Creation Processes. *Journal of Business Venturing Insights* 9:10–16.

Steiner, Christopher. (2010). Startup.com: The Sequel. *Forbes.* 10 July. Accessed online.

U.S. Census, U.S. Department of Commerce. (no date). Quick Facts, accessed May 19, 2017 at www.census.gov/en/html.

U.S. Securities and Exchange Commission. (2013). Facebook, Inc. Form 10-K. ID Number: 10-K 1 fb-12312013x10k.htm 10-K, accessed June 2, 2018 at www.sec.gov.

U.S. Small Business Administration. (2007). The Small Business Economy for Data Year 2006: A Report to the President. Washington, DC: U.S. Government Printing Office.

Wikipedia. (2013). Facebook, accessed 2013 at https://en/wikipedia.org/w/index.php?title-Facebook&oldid=78936914.

Writers Institute. (undated). "Startup.com" film notes. State University of New York at Albany, accessed June 2, 2018 at https://www.albany.edu/writers-inst/webpages4/fimnotes/fns03n8.html.

Xu, Hongwei and Martin Ruef. (2004). The Myth of the Risk-tolerant Entrepreneur. *Strategic Organization* 2(4):331–355.

Index

activity clusters
  creating an infrastructure 91
  funding related efforts 91
  impact of 92
  legal recognition of intellectual
    property 91
  operation of business activity 90
  organizing of start-up team 91
  overview of 95–6
  planning efforts 91
  policy implications of 96
  public presence 90
  relationship with profitability
    91
  see also multiple activity clusters
activity domains and outcomes 91,
  94
allocation, of economic resources
  42
asset backed loans 117
attracting customers 89–90
  significance of 90
autonomy, notion of 30

benefits, of business creation 146,
  151
business administration
  courses and outcomes 74
  skills for 17
business associates 60, 65
business creation 1–2, 49
  benefits of 146
  dominated by immigrants 18
  major issues associated with 10
  overview of 10
  participation in see participation
    in business creation
  policy implications 10–11
  ten things to know about 4

business creators 17, 20, 26, 30, 37,
  38, 40, 42–3, 51, 148
  social networks of 23
business ideas 57, 92, 96, 98, 119,
  128–9, 150, 152
  development of 6, 30
  nascent ventures based on 76
  sources of 70–71
business license 88
business management 74–5, 77, 145
business opportunity 16–17, 23,
  26–8, 32, 43–4, 47, 51, 125, 148
business owners 6, 11, 26–7, 32, 135
  rewards of business ownership 26
  social network of 17
business plan adjustments, reasons
  for 128
business planning 79, 92, 149
business services 7, 61, 63, 65
business skills 61

career
  employment 17
  opportunities 88, 139
case weights, development of
  duration in process adjustment
    156–7
  effect on
    start-up process outcomes 158
    time in start-up process 159
  sample screening adjustment 156
  team size adjustment 156
  triple-adjusted 158
challenges, in business creation 88,
  90
classroom experience 74–5
complications, in business creation
  attracting customers/revenues 89
  financial support 89

169

Printed and bound by CPI Group (UK) Ltd, Croydon, CR0 4YY

23/04/2025

14660982-0001